Virginia Hash

UNI-CENTER FOR MULTICULTURAL EDUCATION
3 6789 62 200308 1

Charles U. Daly-Editor
Charles V. Hamilton
Harold W. Pfautz
Alvin F. Poussaint, M.D.
Richard C. Wade

Urban Violence

**The University
of Chicago
Center for
Policy Study**

DATE DUE

GAYLORD | | | PRINTED IN U.S.A.

D1490315

© The University of Chicago 1969

Previously Published:

* This set may be ordered from The University of Chicago Press, 5750 Ellis Avenue, Chicago, Illinois 60637.

E
185
.U7

TABLE OF CONTENTS

FOREWORD

If violence is not new to our cities, some terms of its occurrence are. They derive from the prison-like slums from which black Americans, unlike their immigrant predecessors, have few means of acquittal.

Quiet frustration is giving way to the cry of the militant. The response is a phrase, code words from the politics of fear:

"Law and Order!"

The things this phrase should mean—law for all, order for all—like the full benefits of American life, remain remote from the millions who inhabit slums.

This booklet presents a brief look at violence in U.S. cities, then discusses how it differs today from that of the past, examines the psychological basis of the urban revolt, and touches upon some of the political and social paths to change.

The papers arise from a conference held by The University of Chicago Center for Policy Study in November, 1967, after a summer that saw portions of Detroit and Newark destroyed. The authors have revised their work since then to take into account more recent events.

Immediately following the conference, the Center published Morris Janowitz's monograph, *Social Control of Escalated Riots*, a paper which he had presented to the conferees. It contained a sociological analysis of the transformation of riots from communal riots—a struggle between members of the white and black communities—to commodity riots—an eruption of the black community against the agents of the larger society. While assessing the conditions that let to riots and the need for fundamental social and political change, Janowitz presented an analysis of how policy action can exaccerbate riots. He emphasized the use of man power rather than fire power when police action becomes necessary. He stressed that "the goal of social control in a political democracy is to enhance the personal competence and personal control of the individual." His paper appeared after 43 persons were killed in the Detroit riot, but prior to the famous Chicago edict "shoot to kill . . . shoot to maim."

Other sessions in the Center's two-year program on urban problems have studied the constitutionality of inequities between public school districts, reviewed the role of the media in dealing with the problems of the cities, examined race and unemployment, and discussed urban design.

Each session has involved the participation of faculty Fellows of the

5

Center and of leaders from public life, as well as other persons from this and other institutions.

Since the Center's first session on urban violence, the National (Kerner) Advisory Commission on Civil Disorders has issued its report, as several of the papers included here note. The Commission's report shocked many Americans, not so much by the recitation of facts and statistics on the imperfections in the society, as by daring to cite "white racism" as a major barrier to political and social change. The Commission predicted that the United States was moving toward two societies, one white and one black. It would have been more accurate to say we are those two societies now, and to point out that we must move from that sad position or face increasingly violent lives in which only some can find liberty, justice, and order.

The contributors to this volume are Richard C. Wade, urban historian; Alvin F. Poussaint, M.D., psychiatrist; Charles Hamilton, political scientist; and Harold Pfautz, sociologist. Each approaches the problem from his discipline. Wade shows the changes in the context in which urban violence occurs. Poussaint examines the outrage of black Americans confronted with the results of white racism. Hamilton appeals for a more equitable distribution of decision-making. Pfautz calls upon white Americans to "act out" their own personal commitments. The question remains, however, whether the commitment is there, whether enough Americans are prepared, psychologically, to eliminate the barriers to social and political change.

Without that deep personal commitment and the transformation of it into action, the society will remain polarized and violent.

Charles U. Daly
Director, The Center for Policy Study
Vice-President, The University of Chicago

VIOLENCE IN THE CITIES: A HISTORICAL VIEW

RICHARD C. WADE
The University of Chicago

Violence is no stranger to American cities. Almost from the very beginning, cities have been the scenes of sporadic violence, of rioting and disorders, and occasionally virtual rebellion against established authority. Many of these events resulted in only modest property damage and a handful of arrests. Others were larger in scale with deaths running into the scores and damages into the millions. This paper attempts to survey briefly some of these outbreaks and to analyze their origins and consequences. We confine ourselves, however, to the larger ones, and omit any discussion of individual acts of violence or the general level of crime. In addition, to keep these remarks relevant to the present crisis, we have confined our analysis to disorders in urban areas.

There has been, in fact, a good deal more violence and disorder in the American tradition than even historians have been willing to recognize. The violence on the frontier is, of course, well known, and in writing, movies, and television it has been a persistent theme in our culture. Indeed, one of America's favorite novelists, James Fenimore Cooper, transformed the slaughter and mayhem of Indians into heroic, almost patriotic, action. As the literary historian David Brion Davis has observed: "Critics who interpret violence in contemporary literature as a symptom of a sick society may be reassured to know that American writers have always been preoccupied with murder, rape, and deadly combat." To be sure, violence is not "as American as cherry pie," but it is no newcomer to the national scene.

Though serious scholarship on this dimension of the American past is shamefully thin, it is already quite clear that disorder and violence in our cities were not simply occasional aberrations, but rather a significant part of urban development and growth. From the Stamp Act riots of the pre-revolutionary age, to the assaults on immigrants and Catholics in the decades before the Civil War, to the grim confrontation of labor and management at the end of the nineteenth century and its sporadic reappearance after World War I and during the depression, through the long series of racial conflicts for two centuries, American cities have known the physical clash of groups, widescale breakdown of established authority, and bloody disorder.

Nor is it hard to see why this early history had more than its share of chaos. American cities in the eighteenth and nineteenth centuries were very young. They had not yet the time to develop a system of orderly government; there was no tradition of habitual consent to local authority; there was no established police system. In addition, these cities grew at a spectacular rate. In the twentieth century, we have used the term "exploding metropolis" to convey the rapid pace of urbanization. It is not often remembered that the first "urban explosion" took place more than a century ago. Indeed, between 1820 and 1860 cities grew proportionately faster than they had before or ever would again. The very speed of this urban development was unsettling and made the maintenance of internal tranquillity more difficult.

The problem was further compounded by the fact that nearly every American city was born of commerce. This meant that there was always a large transient population—seamen engaged in overseas trade, rivermen plying the inland waters, teamsters and wagonmen using the overland routes, and a constant stream of merchants and salesmen seeking customers. At any moment the number of newcomers was large and their attachments to the community slight. Hence when they hit town, there was always some liveliness. After exhausting the cities' museums and libraries, sailors and teamsters would find other things to do. In the eighteenth and nineteenth century, transients comprised a significant portion of those who engaged in rioting and civil disorders.

In addition to being young, rapidly growing, and basically commercial, American cities also had very loose social structures. Unlike the Old World, they had no traditional ruling group, class lines were constantly shifting, and new blood was persistently pumped into these urban societies. One could say that up until the last part of the nineteenth century, mercantile leaders dominated municipal government; but even that commercial leadership changed continually. Later, immigrant groups shared high offices in municipal affairs, thus underlining the shifting nature of the social structure of most cities. Within this looseness there was always a great deal of mobility, with people rising and falling in status not only from generation to generation but within a single lifetime.

This fluid social system contrasted sharply with other, older societies, yet it contained a high incidence of disorder. For it depended on the constant acceptance of new people and new groups to places of influence and importance, and their incorporation into the system on a basis of equality with others. This acceptance was only grudgingly conceded, and often only after some abrasive episodes. The American social structure thus had a large capacity to absorb revolutionary tensions and avoid convulsive upheavals. But it also bred minor social skirmishes which were not always orderly. It is significant that in the pre-Civil War South, where slavery created a more traditional social structure, there was less rioting and civil disorder than in the North (though one ought not underestimate the individual violence against the slave built into institutional bondage).

The American social structure was also unique because it was composed not only of conventional classes, but also of different ethnic, religious, and racial groups. They had at once an internal cohesion that came from a common background and a shared American experience and also a sense of sharp differences with other groups, especially with the country's older stock. These groups, the Negro excepted, were initially both part of the system and yet outside of it. The resultant friction, with the newcomers pressing for acceptance and older groups striving for continued supremacy, was a fruitful source of disorder and often violence. Since it was in the city that these groups were thrown together, became aware of their differences, and struggled for survival and advancement, it would be on the streets rather than on the countryside that the social guerrilla warfare would take place.

If the internal controls in the American social structure were loose, the external controls were weak. The cities inherited no system of police control adequate to the numbers or to the rapid increase of the urban centers. The modern police force is the creation of the twentieth century; the establishment of a genuinely professional system is historically a very recent thing. Throughout the eighteenth and nineteenth century, the force was small, untrained, poorly paid, and part of the political system. In case of any sizable disorder, it was hopelessly inadequate; and rioters sometimes routed the constabulary in the first confrontation. Josiah Quincy, for example, in Boston in the 1820's had to organize and arm the teamsters to re-establish the authority of the city in the streets. Many prudent officials simply kept out of the way until the worst was over. In New York's draft riots, to use another instance, the mayor wandered down to see what the disturbance was all about and nearly got trampled in the melee.

Moreover, since some of the rioting was political, the partisanship of the police led official force to be applied against one group, or protection to be withheld from another. And with every turnover in the mayor's office, a substantial and often a complete change occurred in the police. In Atlanta, for instance, even where there was only one party, each faction had its own men in blue ready to take over with the changes in political fortunes. In some places where the state played a role in local police appointments, the mayor might even be deprived of any control at all for the peace of the city. In New York in the 1850's there was an awkward moment when there were two police forces—the Municipals and the Metropolitans—each the instrument of opposing parties. At the point of the most massive confusion, one group tried to arrest the mayor and an armed struggle took place between the two competing forces.

The evolution toward more effective and professional forces was painfully slow. Separating the police from patronage proved difficult, the introduction of civil service qualifications and protection came only in this century, and the development of modern professional departments came even later. To be sure, after a crisis—rioting, widescale looting, or a crime wave—there would be a demand for reform, but the enthusiasm was seldom sustained and conditions returned quickly to normal. The ultimate safety of the city thus resided with outside forces that could be brought in when local police could not handle the mob.

These general considerations account in large part for the high level of disorder and violence in American cities over the past three centuries. The larger disorders, however, often stemmed from particular problems and specific conditions and resulted in widescale bloodshed and destruction. Though these situations varied from place to place and time to time, it is perhaps useful to divide them into a few categories. Some rioting was clearly political, surrounding party struggles and often occasioned by legislation or an election. Some sprang from group conflict, especially the resistance to the rising influence of immigrant groups. Still others stemmed from labor disputes. And the largest, then as now, came out of race conflict. A few examples of each will convey some of their intensity and scale.

Politics has always been a fruitful source of disorders. Indeed, one of the most significant groups of riots surrounded the colonial break with

Great Britain. In Boston, Samuel Adams and other radical leaders led the otherwise directionless brawling and gang warfare around the docks and wharfs into a political roughhouse against British policy. The Stamp Tax Riots, the Townshend Duty Riots and, of course, the Boston Massacre were all part of an organized and concerted campaign by colonial leaders. The urban middle classes initially tolerated the disorders because they too opposed certain aspects of British policy; they later pulled back when they felt that radical leadership was carrying resistance beyond their own limited objectives. Yet for nearly a decade, rioting and organized physical force was a part of the politics of the colonies.

This use of violence in politics was not as jarring to the eighteenth century as it would be today. Rioting had been a common occurrence, and not always among the underclasses. As early as 1721, Cotton Mather, one of Boston's most prominent citizens, could bewail in his diary the exploits of his "miserable, miserable, miserable son Increase. The wretch has brought himself under public infamy and trouble by bearing a part in a Night-riot, with some detestable rakes in town." Two decades later, Philadelphia witnessed widespread disorder during its "Bloody Election" in 1742. The widening of the franchise greatly reduced the resort to violence in politics for the ballot provided an alternative to rock-throwing and physical force on important public questions. Yet historically the stakes of political victory have always been high enough to induce some to employ force and mob action.

Attacks against immigrants comprise another theme in the story. Often the assault by older, more established groups was against individuals or small groups. But in other cases it would be more general. The string of riots against Catholic churches and convents in the nineteenth century, for example, represented an attack on the symbols of the rise of the new groups. In the summer of 1834, for instance, a Charlestown (Mass.) convent was sacked and burned to the ground; scuffles against the Irish occurred in various parts of nearby Boston; some Irish houses were set afire. At the outset, the episode was carefully managed; then it got out of hand as teenage toughs got into action. Nor was this an isolated incident.

Characteristic of this period too was the resistance to the incorporation of immigrants into the public life of the city. "Bloody Monday" in Louisville in 1855 will perhaps serve as an illustration. Local politicians had become worried about the increase of the immigrant (German and Irish) vote. The Know-Nothings (a party built in part on anti-immigrant attitudes) determined to keep foreign-born residents away from the polls on election day. There was only a single voting place for every ward, thus numbering only eight in the entire city. Know-Nothing followers rose at dawn and occupied the booths early in the morning. They admitted their own reliables, but physically barred their opponents. The pre-election campaign had been tense and bitter with threats of force flying across party lines. By this time some on each side had armed themselves. Someone fired a shot, and the rioting commenced. When it was all through, "Quinn's Row," an Irish section, had been gutted, stores looted, and Catholic churches damaged. A newspaper which was accused of stirring up feeling only barely escaped destruction. The atrocities against the Irish were especially brutal with many being beaten and shot. Indeed, some of the wounded were thrown back into the flames of ignited buildings. Estimates of the dead range from 14 to 100, though historians have generally accepted (albeit with slim evidence) 22 as the number killed.

Labor disputes have also often spawned widescale disorder. Indeed, at the turn of the century, Winston Churchill, already a keen student of American affairs, observed that the United States had the most violent industrial relations of any western country. Most of this rioting started with a confrontation of labor and management over the right to organize, or wages and hours, or working conditions. A large portion of these strikes found the workers in a vulnerable if not helpless position, a fact which has led most historians to come down on the side of labor in these early disputes. Moreover, unlike the disorders we have previously discussed, these were nationwide in scope—occurring at widely scattered points. There was no question of their being directed since a union was usually involved and it had some control over local action throughout the country. Yet the violence was seldom uniform or confined to strikers. It might flare up in Chicago and Pittsburgh, while St. Louis, where the issues would be the same, might remain quiescent. Often, as in the case of the railroad strike of 1877, the damage to life and property was large. In the Homestead lockout alone, 35 were killed and the damage (in 1892 dollars) ran to $2,500.00. In the 1930's the organizing steel, auto, and rubber unions brought a recrudescence of this earlier grisly process.

The "Great Strike of 1877" conveys most of the elements of this kind of violent labor dispute. One historian of the episode observes that "frequently, law and order broke down in major rail centers across the land;

what was regarded as 'domestic insurrection' and 'rebellion' took over."
He calculated that "millions of dollars worth of property were destroyed,
hundreds of persons were injured, and scores killed in rioting in pitched
battles with law enforcement officials." The cities affected stretched
across the country, including Baltimore, Pittsburgh, Philadelphia, Buf-
falo, Cleveland, Toledo, Columbus, Cincinnati, Louisville, Indianapolis,
Chicago, St. Louis, Kansas City, Omaha, and San Francisco.

The strike began on July 16, 1877, in the midst of hard times when
railroads tried to adapt to the depression by cutting wages 10 per cent.
The workers' resistance began in Martinsburg, West Virginia, where the
militia called to the strike scene soon fraternized with the workers. President Rutherford Hayes then dispatched troops to the town and no bloodshed occurred. But in Baltimore, the situation turned ugly and spilled
over into violence on July 20. It is hard to know how many genuine
strikers were involved and how much of the fighting and damage was
done by others. At any rate, 11 people were killed and 20 wounded and
the President again dispatched troops to the troubled area. After these
eruptions, the riots spread elsewhere. One historian describes the subse-
quent disorders as "undirected, unplanned, and unmanaged save by im-
promptu leaders." "Everywhere," he continued, "but especially in Baltimore, Pittsburgh, and Chicago, the striking trainmen were promptly
joined by throngs of excitement seeking adolescents, by the idle, the unemployed, the merely curious and the malicious."

Pittsburgh suffered the worst. As trouble first threatened, the governor
called up the local militia whose members very quickly began to frater-
nize with the strikers as the latter took over the trains. The governor
then called for troops from Philadelphia. In the furious clash that resulted, 16 soldiers and 50 rioters were killed. "For two days Pittsburgh
was ruled by mobs," one account asserts, "which burned, looted and pil-
laged to their heart's content, and attacked savagely all who resisted
them. Finally the riot died out; into harmlessness. The city was left in
ruins." In the last stages, however, the same historian observed that "the
rioting had little or no connection with the strike, and few strikers were
included in the mobs." In addition to the lives lost, property destroyed
included 500 freight cars, 104 locomotives, and 39 buildings.

The strike reached Chicago on July 23. Men left the job and large
crowds began to collect. By nightfall, the city was paralyzed. Police were
dispatched to disperse the throng and in the first clash they fired into

the crowd, killing seven and wounding twenty. The militia arrived and citizens groups began to arm. The superintendent of police estimated that there were 20,000 armed men in Chicago by the second day. On the 26th the United States Army arrived. At 16th Street, 350 police faced a mob of about 6,000 and after an hour's battle at least twelve died and two score or more were seriously wounded. Like most riots, the point of origin and the purpose of the strike were soon forgotten. Indeed, an astute student of the event asserts that "practically none of the rioting may be fairly ascribed to the strikers." Rather, he asserts, "the disturbances were mainly caused by roughs, idlers, unemployed persons, and the criminal element. A surprisingly large percentage of the mobs was composed of women and young boys, and these elements were at the same time the most destructive and the hardest for the police to disperse." He adds, however, that the blame was not one-sided: "It seems also that a good deal of the disturbance was precipitated by the rough tactics of the police."

The Pullman strike in Chicago almost twenty years later also contained most of the familiar elements of a riot growing out of a labor dispute. It, too, stemmed from a wage reduction in the middle of a depression. On May 11, 1894, the strike began in a quiet and orderly fashion. As the gap between the workers and the Pullman Company deepened, the American Railway Union called for a general boycott of sleeping cars. A federal court, however, issued an injunction against the boycott to insure the movement of mail. On July 4 federal troops arrived in Chicago. Until that time a labor historian observed that "there had been little violence in Chicago proper. Some acts of sabotage had occurred and there had been occasional demonstrations but the police had effectively controlled the latter."

Now the temper of the episode changed. Crowds roamed over the tracks "pushing over freight cars, setting a few of them on fire, and otherwise blocking the movement of trains. Switches were thrown, signal lights changed, and trains stoned—much of the trouble caused by half-grown boys who seemed to welcome the opportunity for excitement and deviltry." Furthermore, "a large proportion of women and children" mingled in a crowd that reached 10,000. Adding to the incendiary possibilities was an "abnormally large group of hoodlums, tramps, and semi-criminals, some of whom had been attracted to Chicago by the Columbian Exposition and left stranded by the depression." "In the movement of the mobs," the same historian continues, "there was seldom any purpose or leadership. Most of the destruction was done wantonly and without premeditation."

July 6 was the day of the greatest property destruction. A reporter from the *Inter Ocean* described the scene at the height of the frenzy. "From this moving mass of shouting rioters squads of a dozen or two departed, running towards the yards with fire brands in their hands. They looked in the gloaming like specters, their lighted torches bobbing about like will-o'the-wisps. Soon from all parts of the yard flames shot up and billows of fire rolled over the cars, covering them with the red glow of destruction. The spectacle was a grand one. . . . Before the cars were fired those filled with any cargoes were looted. . . . The people were bold, shameless, and eager in their robbery. . . . It was pandemonium let loose, the fire leaping along for miles, and the men and women became drunk on their excess." By nightfall 700 cars had been destroyed. The next day clashes between the crowd and a hastily organized militia left 4 more dead and 20 wounded. In all, in three chaotic days, 13 people had been killed, 53 seriously wounded, several hundred more hurt and incalculable property damage, not to mention money lost in wages and railroad earnings. One estimate fixes the total at $80,000,000.

Of all the sources of civil disorder, however, none has been more persistent than race. Whether in the North or South, whether before or after the Civil War, whether nineteenth or twentieth century, this question has been at the root of more physical violence than any other. There had been some sporadic slave uprisings before emancipation, the largest being the Nat Turner rebellion in 1831. But most which moved from plot to action occurred on the countryside rather than in the cities. Yet even the fear of a slave insurrection took its toll; in 1822, for instance, Charleston, South Carolina, officials, acting on tips and rumors, hanged 37 Negroes and deported many more for an alleged plot to capture and burn the city. Seven years later, in a free state, whites invaded Cincinnati's "Little Africa" and burned and killed and ultimately drove half the colored residents from town. In the same period mobs also assaulted abolitionists, sometimes killing, otherwise sacking buildings and destroying printing presses.

Even the New York City riot against the draft in 1863 took an ugly racial twist before it had run its course. The events themselves arose out of the unpopularity of the draft and the federal government's call for more men as Lee headed into Pennsylvania. The situation was further complicated by a crisis in the police department as a result of the conflicting claims of command by a Republican mayor and a Democratic governor. The rioting broke out July 13 and the first target was the provost marshal's office. Within a short time 700 people ransacked the building and then set it afire. The crowd would not let the firemen into the area and soon the whole block lay gutted. Later the mob began to spill over into the Negro area where many blacks were attacked and some killed.

The police were helpless as the riot spread. The few clashes with the mob saw the police retreat; the crowd wandered about almost at will. Political leaders did not want to take the consequences for action against the mob, and soon it started to head toward the business district. Slowly the police reorganized, by Tuesday they began to win engagements with the rioters, and in a little while they were able to confine the action to the original area. The mobs were, however, better armed and organized and gave a good account of themselves in pitched battle. On the third day federal troops arrived and the control swung over to the authorities and quiet was restored. But in three days the casualties ran to at least 74 dead and many times that number wounded. The property damage was never accurately added up, but claims against the county exceeded $1,500,000 by 1865.

Emancipation freed the Negro from bondage, but it did not grant him either equality or immunity from white aggression. From the New Orleans riot of 1866, through the long list of racial disorders to the end of World War II with datelines running through Atlanta, Springfield, East St. Louis, Washington, Mobile, Beaumont, Chicago, Detroit, and Harlem, reveal something of the depth of the crisis and the vulnerability of American cities to racial disorders. These riots were on a large scale, involved many deaths, millions of dollars of property damage, and left behind deep scars which have never been fully erased. Most of these riots involved the resort to outside military help for containment; all exposed the thinness of the internal and external controls within our urban society.

In fact, the war had scarcely ended before racial violence erupted in New Orleans. The occasion of the outbreak was a Negro procession to an assembly hall where a debate over enfranchising the blacks was to take place. There was some jostling during the march and a shot fired; but it was only after the arrival at the convention that police and special troops charged the black crowd. In the ensuing struggle Negroes were finally routed, but guns, bricks, and stones were generously used. Many Negroes fell on the spot; others were pursued and killed on the streets trying to escape. Later General Sheridan reported that "at least nine-tenths of the casualties were perpetrated by the police and citizens by stabbing and smashing in the heads of many who had already been wounded or killed by policemen." Moreover, he added that it was not just a riot but "an absolute massacre by the police . . . a murder which the mayor and police . . . perpetrated without the shadow of necessity." Federal troops arrived in the afternoon, took possession of the city, and restored order. But 34 Negroes and 4 whites were already dead and over 200 injured.

Smaller places, even in the North, were also affected with racial disorder. In August 1908, for instance, a three-day riot took its toll in Springfield, Illinois. The Negro population in the capital had grown significantly in the years after the turn of the century, and some whites sensed a political and economic threat. On August 13th a white woman claimed she had been violated by a Negro. An arrest was made and the newspapers carried an inflammatory account of the episode. Crowds gathered around the jail demanding the imprisoned black, but the sheriff quickly transferred the accused and another Negro to a prison in a nearby town without letting the public know. "The crowd outside was in an ugly mood," writes an historian of the riot, "the sun had raised tempers; many of the crowd had missed their dinners, which added to their irritation; and the authorities seemed to be taking no heed of their presence. By sundown the crowd had become an ugly mob."

The first target of the rioters was a restaurant whose proprietor presumably had driven the prisoners from jail. Within a few minutes his place was a shambles. They then headed for the Negro section. Here they hit homes and businesses either owned by or catering to Negroes. White owners quickly put white handkerchiefs in their windows to show their race; their stores were left untouched. A Negro was found in his shop and was summarily lynched. Others were dragged from streetcars and beaten. On the 15th the first of 5,000 national guardsmen reached Springfield; very quickly the mob broke up and the town returned to normal. The death toll reached six (four whites and two blacks); the property damage was significant. As a result of the attack, Springfield's

Negro population left the city in large numbers hoping to find better conditions elsewhere, especially in Chicago.

A decade later the depredations in East St. Louis were much larger, with the riot claiming the lives of 39 Negroes and 9 whites. The best student of this episode points out that the 1917 riot was not a sudden explosion but resulted from "threats to the security of whites brought on by the Negroes' gains in economic, political and social status; Negro resentment of the attempts to 'kick him back in his place'; and the weakness of the external forces of constraint—the city government, especially the police department." Tensions were raised when the Aluminum Ore Company replaced white strikers with Negro workers. In addition to these factors, race had become a political issue in the previous year when the Democrats accused Republicans of "colonizing" Negroes to swing the election in East St. Louis. The kindling seemed only to lack the match.

On May 28 came the fire. A Central Trades and Labor Union delegation formally requested the Mayor to stop the immigration of Negroes to East St. Louis. As the men were leaving City Hall they heard a story that a Negro robber had accidentally shot a white man during a holdup. In a few minutes the word spread; rumor replaced fact. Now it was said the shooting was intentional; that a white woman was insulted; that two white girls were shot. By this time 3,000 people had congregated and the cry for vengeance went up. Mobs ran downtown beating every Negro in sight. Some were dragged off the streetcars, others chased down. The police refused to act except to take the injured to hospitals and to disarm Negroes. The next day the National Guard arrived to restore order.

Two days later the governor withdrew troops although tension remained high. Scattered episodes broke the peace, but no sustained violence developed. The press, however, continued to emphasize Negro crimes and a skirmish broke out between white pickets and black workers at the Aluminum Company. Then on July 1 some whites drove through the main Negro neighborhood firing into homes. The colored residents armed themselves, and when a similar car, this time carrying a plain-clothesman and reporter, went down the street the blacks riddled the passing auto with gunshot.

The next day was the worst. At about 10:00 A.M. a Negro was shot on the main street and a new riot was underway. An historian of the event asserted that the area along Collinsville Avenue between Broadway and

Illinois Avenue became a "bloody half mile" for three or four hours. "Streetcars were stopped: Negroes, without regard to age or sex, were pulled off and stoned, clubbed and kicked. . . . By the early afternoon, when several Negroes were beaten and lay bloodied in the street, mob leaders calmly shot and killed them. After victims were placed in an ambulance, there was cheering and handclapping." Others headed for the Negro section and set fire to homes on the edge of the neighborhood. By midnight the South End was in flames and black residents began to flee the city. In addition to the dead, the injured were counted in the hundreds and over 300 buildings were destroyed.

Two summers later the racial virus felled Chicago. Once again, mounting tension had accompanied the migration of blacks to the city. The numbers jumped from 44,000 in 1910 to 109,000 ten years later. Though the job market remained good, housing was tight. Black neighborhoods could expand only at the expense of white ones, and everywhere the transition areas were filled with trouble. Between July 1, 1917, and March 1921, there had been 58 bombings of Negro houses. Recreational areas also witnessed continual racial conflict.

The riot itself began on Sunday, July 27, on the 29th Street Beach. There had been some stone-throwing and sporadic fighting. Then a Negro boy, who had been swimming in the Negro section, drifted into the white area and drowned. What happened is not certain, but the young blacks charged he had been hit by stones and demanded the arrest of a white. The police refused, but then arrested a Negro at a white request. When the Negroes attacked the police, the riot was on. News of the events on the beach spread to the rest of the city. Sunday's casualties were 2 dead and 50 wounded. On Monday, attacks were made on Negroes coming from work; in the evening cars drove through black neighborhoods with whites shooting from the windows. Negroes retaliated by sniping at any white who entered the Black Belt. Monday's accounting found 20 killed and hundreds wounded. Tuesday's list was shorter, a handful dead, 139 injured. Wednesday saw a further waning and a reduction in losses in life and property. Rain began to fall; the Mayor finally called in the state militia. After nearly a week a city which witnessed lawlessness and warfare, quieted down and began to assess the implications of the grisly week.

The Detroit riot of 1943 perhaps illustrates the range of racial disorders that broke out sporadically during World War II. There had been earlier conflicts in Mobile, Los Angeles, and Beaumont, Texas, and there would be some others later in the year. No doubt the war with its built-in anxieties and accelerated residential mobility accounted for the timing of these outbreaks. In Detroit, the wider problem was compounded by serious local questions. The Negro population in the city had risen sharply, with over 50,000 arriving in the 15 months before the riot; this followed a historical increase of substantial proportions which saw black residents increase from 40,000 to 120,000 in the single decade between 1920 and 1930. These newcomers put immense pressures on the housing market, and neighborhood turnover at the edge of the ghetto bred bitterness and sometimes violence; importantly, too, recreational areas became centers of racial abrasiveness.

On June 20 the riot broke out on Belle Isle, a recreational spot used by both races, but predominantly by Negroes. Fistfighting on a modest basis soon escalated, and quickly a rising level of violence spread across the city. The Negro ghetto—ironically called Paradise Valley—saw the first wave of looting and bloodshed. The area was, as its historians have described it, "spattered with blood and littered with broken glass and ruined merchandise. The black mob had spared a few shops owned by Negroes who had chalked COLORED on their windows. But almost every store in the ghetto owned by a white had been smashed open and ransacked." Other observers noted that "crudely organized gangs of Negro hoodlums began to operate more openly. Some looters destroyed property as if they had gone berserk."

The next morning saw the violence widen. The police declared the situation out of control and the mayor asked for state troops. Even this force was ineffective, and finally the Governor asked for federal help. Peace returned under the protection of 6,000 men; and the troops remained for more than a week. The dead numbered 34, 25 Negroes and 9 whites; property damage exceeded $2,000,000. And almost as costly was the bitterness, fear, and hate that became part of the city's legacy.

This survey covers only some of the larger and more important disorders. Others reached significant proportions but do not fall into convenient categories. For example, in the eighteenth century a protest against inoculation led to widespread rioting; mobs hit the streets to punish men who snatched bodies for medical training. In times of economic hardship, "bread riots" resulted in ransacking stores; crowds often physically drove away officials seeking to evict tenants who could not pay rent.

Two disorders perhaps best suggest the miscellaneous and unpredictable character of this process. One is so bizarre that only its bloody climax has kept it from being among the most amusing episodes of American history. It revolved around the rivalry between two prominent actors, the American Edwin Forrest, and William Macready, an Englishman. Both were appearing in "Macbeth" on the same night, May 7, 1849, in New York City. Some rowdies, mostly Irish, decided to break up the Macready performance, and when he appeared on the stage they set up such a din that he had to retire. After apologies and assurances, the English visitor agreed to try again on the 9th. This time, the police extracted the troublemakers and Macready finished the play. But a mob gathered outside after the final curtain and refused to disperse on police orders. Finally, the edgy guard fired into the crowd, killing 25 persons.

Another dimension is revealed in the events of March 1884, in Cincinnati. They came in the midst of what the city's best historian has dubbed "the decade of disorder." Two men were tried for the murder of a white livery man. Though one was Negro and the other German, race does not seem to be at issue. When the German was found guilty of only manslaughter, a public campaign developed to avenge the decision. A meeting at Music Hall, called by some leading citizens, attracted 10,000 people, mostly from the middle class, who were worried about a general breakdown of law and order and thought the light sentence would encourage criminals. The speakers attacked the jury and the administration of justice in the city. Afterward a crowd headed for the jail. In the first encounter with the police, casualties were light. But the next day the militia moved in and hostility climbed. Finally, a pitched battle ensued in which 54 died and over 200 were wounded. Thus, a meeting called to bring about law and order wound up ironically in disorder and violence.

This survey, which is only suggestive and not exhaustive, indicates that widescale violence and disorder have been man's companion in the American city from the outset. Some generalizations out of this experience might be useful in the light of the present crisis.

First, most of the rioting has usually been either limited in objective or essentially sporadic. This, of course, is not true of racial conflict, but it is characteristic of a large number of the others. In those, the event was discreet; there was no immediate violent sequel. After a labor dispute, especially if it involved union recognition, bitterness and hate persisted, but there was no annual recurrence of the violence. Attacks on immi-

21

grants seldom produced an encore, though they might have an analogue in some other city in the same month or year. In short, though there was enough disorder and mob action to create a persistent anxiety, the incidence of overt conflict was irregular enough to preclude predictions of the next "long hot summer."

Second, this sporadic quality meant that the postmortems were usually short and shallow. It was characteristic to note the large number of teenagers who got involved; to attribute the disruption to outsiders (especially anarchists and communists); to place a large responsibility on the newspapers for carrying inflammatory information and spreading unfounded rumors; to blame the local police for incompetence, for prejudice, for intervening too soon or too late, or at all. After any episode, the urge to fix blame led to all kinds of analyses. The historian of the 1877 railroad violence, for example, observes that "the riots were variously ascribed to avarice, the expulsion of the Bible from the schools, the protective tariff, the demonetization of silver, the absence of General Grant, the circulation of the *Chicago Times* and original sin." Others saw in it a labor conspiracy or a communist plot. And the *New York Times* could assert after the Chicago riot in 1919 that: "The outbreak of race riots in Chicago, following so closely on those reported from Washington, shows clearly enough that the thing is not sporadic (but has) . . . intelligent direction and management . . . (It seems probable) that the Bolshevist agitation has been extended among the Negroes."

There were a few exceptions. After the Chicago race riot, for example, an Illinois commission studied the event in some detail and also examined the deteriorating relations between the races which lay at the bottom. Others occasionally probed beneath the surface at the deeper causes of unrest. But most cities preferred to forget as soon as possible and hoped for an end to any further disorder. Indeed, even the trials that followed most riots show how rapidly popular interest faded. The number of people brought to trial was small and the number of convictions extremely small; and, most significantly, there was little clamor for sterner measures.

Third, if the analyses of the riots were shallow, the response of cities and legislatures was not very effective. After quiet was restored, there would almost certainly be a discussion of police reform. Customarily little came of it, though in Louisville the utter ineptness and obvious partisanship of the police in 1855 prompted a change from an elective to an appointive force. Legislation usually emphasized control. As early as 1721, Massachusetts responded to growing disorders with an anti-riot act. And Chicago's Commercial Club made land available for Fort Sheridan after the events of 1877 in order to have troops nearby for the protection of the city. But most cities rocked back to normal as soon as the tremors died down.

Fourth, there was a general tendency to rely increasingly on outside forces for containing riots. Partly, this resulted from the fact that in labor disorders local police and even state militia fraternized with strikers and could not be counted on to discipline the workers. Partly, it was due to inadequate numbers in the face of the magnitude of the problem. Partly, too, it stemmed from the fact that sometimes the police were involved in the fighting at the outset and seemed a part of the riot. The first resort was usually to state troops; but they were often unsatisfactory, and the call for federal assistance became more frequent.

Fifth, while it is hard to assess, it seems that the bitterness engendered by riots and disorders was not necessarily irreparable. Though the immigrants suffered a good deal at the hands of nativists, it did not slow down for long the process of their incorporation into American life. Ten years after Louisville's "Bloody Monday" the city had a German mayor. The trade unions survived the assaults of the nineteenth century and a reduction of tension characterized the period between 1900 and the depression (with the notable exception of the post-war flare-ups). And after the violence of the 1930's, labor and management learned to conduct their differences, indeed their strikes, with reduced bloodshed and violence. It is not susceptible of proof, but it seems that the fury of the defeated in these battles exacted a price on the victors that ultimately not only protected the group but won respect, however grudgingly, from the public.

At any rate the old sources of major disorders, race excepted, no longer physically agitate American society. It has been many years since violence has been a significant factor in city elections and no widespread disorders have even accompanied campaigning. Immigrant groups have now become so incorporated in American life that they are not easily visible and their election to high offices, indeed the highest, signals a muting of old hostilities. Even when people organized on a large scale against minority groups—such as the Americans' Protective Association in the 1890's or the Ku Klux Klan in the 1920's—

they have seldom been able to create major riots or disorders. And though sporadic violence occasionally breaks out in a labor dispute, what is most remarkable is the continuance of the strike as a weapon of industrial relations with so little resort to force. Even the destruction of property during a conflict has ceased to be an expectation.

Sixth, race riots were almost always different from other kinds of disorders. Their roots went deeper; they broke out with increasing frequency; and their intensity mounted rather than declined. And between major disorders the incidence of small-scale violence was always high. Until recently, the Negro has largely been the object of the riot. This was true not only in northern cities where changing residential patterns bred violence, but also in the South where this question was less pervasive. In these riots the lines were sharply drawn against the Negroes, the force was applied heavily against them, and the casualties were always highest among blacks.

Finally, in historical perspective, if racial discord be removed, the level of large-scale disorder and violence is less ominous today than it has been during much of the past. As we have seen, those problems which have produced serious eruptions in the past no longer do so. In fact, if one were to plot a graph, omitting the racial dimension, violence and disorder over a long period have been reduced. Indeed, what makes the recent rioting so alarming is that it breaks so much with this historical trend and upsets common expectations.

Yet to leave out race is to omit the most important dimension of the present crisis. For it is race that is at the heart of the present discord. Some analysts, of course, have argued that the problem is class and they emphasize the numbers caught in widening poverty, and the frustration and envy of poor people in a society of growing affluence. Yet it is important to observe that though 68 per cent of the poor people in this country are white, the disorders stem almost wholly from black ghettoes. The marginal participation of a few whites in Detroit and elsewhere scarcely dilutes the racial foundations of these disorders.

In fact, a historical survey of disorders only highlights the unique character of the present problem. For the experience of the Negro in American cities has been quite different from any other group. And it is in just this difference that the crisis lies. Because the black ghetto is unlike any ghettoes that our cities have known before. Of course, other groups knew the ghetto experience too. As newcomers to the city they huddled in the downtown areas where they met unspeakably congested conditions, occupied the worst housing, got the poorest education, toiled, if fortunate enough to have a job, at the most menial tasks, endured high crime rates, and knew every facet of deprivation.

The urban slum had never been a very pleasant place, and it was tolerable only if the residents, or most of them, thought there was a way out. To American immigrants generally the ghetto was a temporary stage in their incorporation into American society. Even some of the first generation escaped, and the second and third generation moved out of the slums in very large numbers. Soon they were dispersed around the metropolitan area, in the suburbs as well as the pleasant residential city wards. Those who remained behind in the old neighborhoods did so because they chose to, not because they had to. By this process, millions of people from numberless countries, of different national and religious backgrounds made their way into the main current of American life.

It was expected that Negroes would undergo the same process when they came to the city. Thus, there was little surprise in the first generation when black newcomers did indeed find their way into the central city, the historic staging grounds for the last and poorest arrivals. But the ghetto proved to be not temporary. Instead of colored residents dispersing in the second generation, the ghetto simply expanded. Block by block it oozed out into the nearby white neighborhoods. Far from breaking up, the ghetto grew. In fact, housing became more segregated every year; and the walls around it appeared higher all the time. What had been temporary for other groups seemed permanent to Negroes.

The growth of the Negro ghetto created conditions which had not existed before and which generated the explosiveness of our present siutation. In the first place, the middle-class Negroes became embittered at their exclusion from the decent white neighborhoods of the city and suburbs. These people, after all, had done what society expected of them; they got their education, training, jobs, and income. Yet even so they were deprived of that essential symbol of American success—the home in a neighborhood of their own choosing where conditions would be more pleasant and schools better for their children. For this group, now about a third of all urban Negroes, the exclusion seemed especially cruel and harsh.

As a result they comprise now a growingly alienated and embittered group. The middle-class blacks are now beginning to turn their attention to organizing among the poor in the worst parts of the ghetto. Their children make up the cadres of black militants in the colleges. And when the riots come, they tolerate the activity even though they usually do not themselves participate. In short, the fact of the ghetto forces them to identify with race, not class. When the riots break, they feel a bond with the rioters, not white society. This had not been true of the emerging middle class of any immigrant group before.

If the ghetto has new consequences for the middle class, it also creates a new situation among the poorer residents of the ghetto, especially for the young people. They feel increasingly that there is no hope for the future. For other groups growing up in the ghetto there had always been visible evidence that it was possible to escape. Many before had done it; and everyone knew it. This produced the expectation that hard work, proper behavior, some schooling, and a touch of luck would make it possible to get ahead. But the young Negro grows up in increasing despair. He asks himself—"What if I do all they say I should—stay in school, get my training, find a job, accumulate some money—I'll still be living here, still excluded from the outside world and its rewards." He asks himself, "What's the use?" Thus, the hopelessness, despair, and frustration mounts, and the temperature of the ghetto rises. Nearly all of our poverty programs are stumbling on the problem of motivation. To climb out of the slum has always required more than average incentive. Yet this is precisely what is lacking in the ghetto youth.

The present riots stem from the peculiar problems of the ghetto. By confining Negroes to the ghetto we have deprived them of the chance to enter American society on the same terms as other groups before them. And they know increasingly that this exclusion is not a function of education, training, or income. Rather, it springs from the color of their skin. This is what makes race the explosive question of our time; this is what endangers the tranquillity of our cities. In the historian's perspective, until the ghetto begins to break, until the Negro middle class can move over this demeaning barrier, until the young people can see Negroes living where their resources will carry them and hence get credible evidence of equality, the summers will remain long and hot.

THE PSYCHOLOGY OF A MINORITY GROUP WITH IMPLICATIONS FOR SOCIAL ACTION

Alvin F. Poussaint, M.D.

Tufts University School of Medicine

Much has been written about the black man's psychic reactions to being a member of an oppressed minority in a white man's land. The position of the Negro is unique among minority groups in America because he alone bears the scars of a slave heritage and wears the indelible mark of oppression—his dark skin. It is impossible in this short paper to discuss all the aspects and implications of the Negro's psychological adaptation to white racism. Therefore, in view of the national crisis in race relations and the black rebellions taking place in our cities, I would like to focus on what I consider those key aspects of the psychology of black Americans having special relevance for the formulation of programmatic solutions to the urban crisis.

The system of slavery in its original form and as its remnants exist today had three dramatic consequences for the black man's psyche. It generated in him 1) self-hatred and negative self-esteem; 2) suppressed aggression and rage; and 3) dependency and non-assertiveness. Although these manifestations are analytically distinguishable, they are of course not discrete phenomena, being interdependent and interrelated on many different levels. Thus, while we will deal with each in turn, a consideration of one necessarily involves reference to the others. (It should be understood that we are here dealing in generalities and that any individual could of course respond differently from what we see as predominant trends.)

Let us briefly look at the genesis and initial consequences of racism and examine Negroes' responses to it.

The castration of Afro-Americans and the resulting problems of negative self-image, suppressed aggression, and dependency started more than 350 years ago when black men, women, and children were wrenched from their native Africa, stripped bare both physically and psychologically, and placed in an alien white land. They thus came to occupy the most degraded of human conditions, that of a slave: a piece of property, a non-person. Families were broken—black men were emasculated and black women were systematically exploited sexually and otherwise vilely degraded. The plantation system implanted and fostered the growth of a helplessness and subserviency in the minds of Negroes that made them dependent upon the goodwill and paternalism of the white man.* The more acquiescent the slave was, the more he was rewarded within the plantation culture. This practice forced the suppression of felt retaliatory rage and aggression in black men and women. Those who bowed and scraped for the white boss and denied their aggressive feelings were promoted to "house nigger" and "good nigger." Thus, within this system, it became a virtue for the black man to be docile and non-assertive. "Uncle Toms" are exemplars of these conditioned virtues. In order to retain the most menial of jobs and keep from starving, black people quickly learned such servile responses as "Yassuh, Massa." Thus, from the days of slavery to the present, passivity (and the resultant dependency) became a necessary survival technique.

By 1863, when slavery was abolished, the Afro-American had been stripped of his culture and left an oppressed black man in a hostile white man's world. He had furthermore learned to repress his aggression, behave subserviently, and view himself as an inferior. These things had been inculcated under the duress of slavery. All of these teachings were, however, reinforced after "freedom" when Jim Crow was born in the late 1800's and early 1900's. In the days following the Reconstruction, the systematized racist and sometimes psychotic propaganda of the white man, haranguing about the inferiority of the Negro, increased in intensity. He was disfranchised, terrorized, mutilated, and lynched. The black man became every unacceptable, pernicious idea and impulse that the white man's psyche wished to project; i.e., the Negro was an animal, violent, murderous, with ravaging sexual impulses. The intensity of the white man's psychological need that the Negro be shaped in the image of this projected mental sickness was such as to inspire the whole Jim Crow system of organized discrimination, segregation, and exclusion of Negroes from society.

In the resulting color caste system, white supremacists constructed an entire "racial etiquette" constantly to remind Negroes that they are only

---

* The present welfare system is in many ways analogous to this system in that it perpetuates this psychological dependency.

castrated humans. In their daily lives, Negroes are called "girl" and "boy" by whites. In the South, in particular, they are addressed by their first name by whites no matter how lowly that white person is. Negroes in turn are, however, expected to use courtesy titles such as Mr., Mrs., or Miss when addressing whites. White racists through the centuries have perpetrated violence on those blacks who demonstrate aggressiveness or insubordination. To be an "uppity nigger" was considered by white supremacists one of the gravest violations of the racial etiquette. Negro mothers learned to instruct their two and three year old children to "behave" and say " 'yes, sir and no, sir' when the white man talks to you." Similarly, various forms of religious worship in the Negro community have fostered passivity in blacks and encouraged them to look to an after-life for eventual salvation and happiness. Negroes have even been taught that they must love their oppressors and that it is "sinful" to hate or show appropriate anger.

In addition to demanding non-aggression and subservience, whites also inculcated in the Negro low self-esteem and self-hatred. They made certain that any wares allotted to the Negro were inferior. The Caucasian American socialized the black man to internalize and believe the many deprecating things which were said about him. They encouraged and rewarded behavior and attitudes in Negroes that substantiated these indicting stereotypes. Thus black men were happy-go-lucky and were laughed at by whites. Negroes were lazy, stupid, and irresponsible, and whites bemoaned this, but "put up with it" in a good-natured "noblesse oblige" fashion. Our mass media vigorously reinforced these images with such characters as Amos and Andy, Stepin Fetchit, and Beulah. In this way many Negroes were conditioned to believe, "Yes, I am inferior."

Not only were black men taught that black was evil and that Negroes were "no-good," they were also continually brainwashed into believing that only "white is right." This psychological feat was accomplished by allowing light-skinned Negroes with straight hair to elevate themselves in society above darker Negroes. As this happened, the whites suggested, and Negroes came to believe, that such blacks were better because they had much "white blood." Thus, for the darker Negroes, their lack of social and economic success and their deprived conditions came to be associated with their Negroid qualities. Consequently Negroes exhibited profound shame in the vestiges of their African identity and sought to hide or deny these. Without the positive history of their former African culture and its achievements to raise their self-esteem, and with the achievements of both the white men and the "whiter Negroes" staring them in the face, black men sought to be white. They revered characteristics which were Caucasian—pale skins, straight hair, aquiline features—and despised their own curly hair, broad noses, and full lips.

The most tragic, yet predictable, part of all of this structuring is that the Negro has come to form his self-image and self-concept on the basis of what white racists have prescribed. Therefore, black men and women learn quickly to hate themselves and each other because they are black.

These, then, are the broad historical outlines of certain aspects of the black man's situation in the United States—those related to his socialization in an oppressive system and having consequences for his psychological development. We have briefly discussed those patterned and institutionalized stimuli present over the years in black-white interaction which gave rise in the Negro to such learned habits of response as self-hatred and negative self-esteem, suppressed rage, and subserviency. In the next section we shall explore some of the more critical dynamics and manifestations of these characteristics, focusing especially on those having implications for social action planning.

Although the Negro's self-concept is affected by factors associated with poverty and low economic class status, blackness in itself has consequences for ego development which are not inherent in lower-class membership. The black person develops in a color caste system and usually acquires the negative self-esteem that is the natural outcome of membership in the lowest stratum of such a system. Through contact with such institutionalized symbols of caste inferiority as segregated schools, neighborhoods, and jobs and more indirect negative indicators such as the reactions of his own family, he gradually becomes aware of the social and psychological implications of his racial membership. He is likely to see himself as an object of scorn and disparagement, unwelcome in a white high caste society and unworthy of love and affection. The young Negro child learns very early in life to despise himself and to reject those like himself. From that time on his entire personality and style of interaction with his environment become molded and shaped in a warped, self-hating, and self-denigrating way.

Sometimes this self-hatred can take on very subtle manifestations. For instance, competition, which may bring success, may also bring failure. Thus, the efforts which may bring success to a black man are often not made even when the opportunity exists. This is no doubt for two reasons: First, the anxiety that accompanies growth and change is avoided if a new failure is not risked; therefore a try is not made. Second, the steady state of failure represented by non-achievement (and defined by someone other than yourself) rather than by an unsuccessful trial, is what many Negroes have come to know and expect, and so they feel safer (less psychologically discomforted) with the more familiar. Furthermore, it has often meant survival to black men to deny the possession of brains, thoughts, and feelings, thus making it difficult to move from a position of passivity to one of activity and to acknowledge heretofore forbidden feelings and behavior as now safe, legitimate, and acceptable.

It is all too frequent that Negroes with ability, intelligence, and talent do not aspire to the full extent of their potential. Being unused to occupying positions of prestige and responsibility, many Afro-Americans have lower aspirations than their talents and abilities warrant. They tend to shy away from competition, particularly with white people and often feel insecure even when their abilities and success have been acknowledged. In fact, at least one study has demonstrated that even when Negroes are given objective evidence of their equal intellectual ability in an interracial situation they typically continue to feel inadequate and to react submissively[1]. This lack of aggressiveness may also account at least in part for Negroes' below par achievement in school. Negro girls, however, who are not as threatening to whites and therefore not as systematically crushed as Negro boys, have been found to exceed Negro boys in achievement at all grade levels through college[2]. Thus their low aspirations and achievement may be due not only to their own feelings of inferiority, but also to a learned inability to be normally aggressive. Many psychiatrists feel that self-denigration in Negroes is associated primarily with the more general castration of the black man by white society. Some even believe that the self-hatred should be viewed as *rage* turned inward rather than as primarily their shame in being black and their desire to be white. Let us look further at this relationship of rage to self-hatred.

Even if a Negro does not start out with self-hatred feelings, these can develop from compromising with a suppressive society.

A Negro with all the self-love and self-confidence in the world cannot express legitimate feelings of anger or rage in a system that is brutally and unstintingly suppressive of self-assertion. Therefore, after a while even a confident Negro would have to hate himself for biting his tongue and not expressing himself in an appropriate way. Even though talking back to a white man, in the South, for example, may mean his life and keeping quiet is the most sensible self-preservatory response, a person has to hate not only the person who forces him to be silent, but also *himself* for acquiescing and compromising his integrity. This is the self-hatred that comes from a feeling of helplessness and powerlessness in the face of overwhelming oppression. The whole system of Southern legal justice has been designed—and still functions—to inflict severe and inequitable penalties on Negroes showing even minor aggression toward whites. Negroes who dare to show their anger at whites are usually punished out of proportion to their "crime." Even in the North, blacks who are "too outspoken" about racial injustices often lose their jobs or are not promoted to higher positions because they are considered "unreasonable" or "too sensitive." It is significant that the civil rights movement had to adopt passive-resistance and non-violence in order to win acceptance by white America. But, alas, even here, there was too much "aggression" shown by Negroes. Whites recoiled and accused civil rights groups of "provoking violence" by peaceful protest.

These responses are of course related to tendencies to be dependent and subservient. The inability of Negroes to be self-assertive has fostered a dependency which has had devastating consequences for the social behavior and psychic responses of Negroes. It has been found, for instance, that Negroes are less likely to go into business or entrepreneurial ventures[3]. This is due no doubt to a trained incapacity to be assertive—a quality essential to the entrepreneurial spirit. For example, a Negro may be afraid to make a decision without checking with a white man, or unless whites approve of his decision.

The demands of being unwillingly subservient, unwillingly self-denigrating, and unwillingly non-aggressive are psychically extremely taxing. Frustration and anger are the obvious by-products of the requirement to be less than a man—less than human. Thus, we come to an obvious question: What does the black man do with his anger and aggression?

The simplest method for dealing with rage is to suppress it and substitute an opposing emotional attitude—compliance, docility, or a "loving attitude." Sometimes anger can be denied completely and replaced by a compensatory happy-go-lucky disposition, flippancy, or—an attitude extremely popular among Negroes—"being cool." Another way for aggression to be channeled is through competitive sports, music, or dancing. These are the few activities which white society has traditionally opened to Negroes. Another acceptable means of channeling rage is to identify with the oppressor and put all of one's energy into striving to be like him. A third means for the oppressed to give expression to their feelings is to empathize or identify with someone objectively like themselves (black), who for one reason or another is free to express appropriate rage directly at the oppressor. Malcolm X and Adam Clayton Powell served this function. Still another technique for dealing with anger is to replace it with a type of chronic resentment and stubbornness toward white people—interpreted as a "chip on the shoulder." Trying to control rage in this way frequently shows itself in a general irritability and always has the potential of becoming explosive. Thus, the spreading wave of riots in Negro ghettos may be seen as outbursts of suppressed rage. Although these riots are contained in the ghetto, the hatred is usually directed at those whom the rioters see as controlling and oppressing them economically, psychologically, and physically—store owners and policemen.

Sometimes suppressed emotions will be expressed in such psychosomatic symptoms as headaches, low back pain, and diarrhea. Rage is also directed inward in such deviations as alcoholism, drug addiction, and excessive gambling, and also in the tendency to distrust and hate other blacks more than they do their white oppressors. In psychiatric practice it is a generally accepted principle that a chronic repressed rage will eventually lead to a low self-esteem, depression, emotional dullness, and apathy.

It appears now as if more and more Negroes are freeing themselves of suppressed rage through greater outspoken release of pent-up emotions. Perhaps this is an indication that self-love is beginning to outbalance self-hate in the black man's soul. The old passivity is fading and being replaced by a drive to undo centuries of powerlessness, helplessness, and dependency under American racism.

If we believe that self-hatred, suppressed rage, non-assertiveness, and dependency are at the core of many of the black man's social and psychological difficulties, what can *American society* do to remove some of these scars from the black psyche? What programs in the black community itself will foster a positive self-image, channel rage, and encourage constructive self-assertion? The answers to these questions are obviously not simple ones and perhaps they will require a serious examination of the basic value system of American society. But some answers are suggested by a consideration of the consequences of the two major philosophies underlying social action programs designed to change the position of the Negro in the United States. There are, first, those whose aims are integration of the black man into society and, second, those which aim to improve the position of the black man in society, but do not emphasize his integration into it. Let us first look at the integrationist orientation.

The civil rights gains in the past decade, and especially in the 1960's, have done much to modify the negative self-concepts of Afro-Americans. The civil rights movement itself has brought a new sense of dignity and respect to those blacks most severely deprived by poverty and oppression in the rural South and Northern ghetto. One factor which may have been significant in improving the self-image of the masses of Negroes was that black men were leading this struggle, rather than white men. This fact in itself probably made Negroes, through the process of identification, take more pride in their group and feel less helpless; for they could see black men, through *their* efforts, knowing more and bringing about positive changes in their environment. The feeling of "fate control," that is, that one can have "control" over social forces rather than be a victim of them, is crucial to one's feelings of ego-strength and self-esteem. Thus, the movement brought to the Negro a new sense of power in a country dominated by a resistant white majority. The movement also acted to channel the expressions of assertiveness among Negroes even if this expression came mainly through non-violent protest. Beyond these achievements, however, civil rights leaders at that time tended to see total integration of the black and white races as the final step in destroying the Negro's negative self-esteem and dependency on white authority.

Now we have seen emerge in segments of the civil rights movement a disenchantment with the social and psychological consequences of American "integration." This disenchantment arises, at least in part, from the fact that integration has moved at a snail's pace and has been marked by white resistance and tokenism. The Negro has found himself in the demeaning and uncomfortable position of asking and demanding that the white man let him into *his* schools, *his* restaurants, *his* theaters, even though he knows that the white man did not want him. In the South and North, many Afro-Americans have resented the indignity of constantly being in the position of "begging for acceptance" into the white man's institutions. Such a posture placed blacks in the same old dependent relationship to the white man as when he asked for and expected food and protection from the slave master. Negroes have become further demoralized upon seeing that the recent civil rights laws did not effectively change this pattern of relationships with whites. It immediately became apparent that integration, especially in schools, was not to be integration in a real sense at all, but merely token placement of Negro children—that is "one-way integration." Negro parents in the South and North for example rarely speak of sending their children to the "integrated school," they say, "My child is going to the *white* school." In the overwhelming majority of instances, no white children are "integrated" into Negro schools. Since integration is only a one-way street that Negroes travel to a white institution, then inherent in the situation itself is the implied inferiority of the black man and the fact that *he* must seek out whites to better his position. This implies that only he can benefit and learn, that he has nothing to offer whites and they have nothing to learn from him. Thus an already negative self-image is reinforced.

Parents who fear psychological harm to their children are not anxious to send them to "integrated" schools. Some of the college-aged young people in the movement stated frankly that they find this type of integration personally degrading and do not want to go any school where they have to be "accepted by white racists." It must be remembered that black people are seeking not only social and economic help but psychological salvation. The Negro is not only demanding equal rights but is desperately searching for *inner* emancipation and escape from the chronic effects of white racism upon his psyche. In this search for peace many young blacks (even on our college campuses) feel a need to insulate themselves from the subtle expressions of racism which they experience in their daily encounters with whites. In this context the growth of black organizations on campuses takes on a significance notably different from the one of "racist separatism" often imputed by the press. Perhaps this isolation serves to protect them from feelings of self-consciousness which they experience in the presence of whites. Such uncomfortable feelings prevent them from feeling relaxed and thus "being themselves."

Since the number of Negroes at any white school is token, particular hardships are created for these individuals. They immediately find themselves surrounded by children who are generally the products of white racist homes. In this situation, since all children want to belong, the Negro must become an expert at "being liked and accepted." In such a social setting, if the self-esteem of the black student grows, it is likely to be not so much from feelings of comfort and satisfaction in being Negro as it is from his own conditioned beliefs that "white is right" and that he has succeeded in a white world; thus he is either a successful pioneer or a martyr.

Those people who offer assimilation as a solution must examine what they are asking Negroes to do. Many Negroes, including segments of both the old civil rights movement and nationalists, are beginning to fear that "token integration" may augment the identity problems of the Negro. Such integration as has existed in the North has not substantially helped to solve the Negro's identity problems. Assimilation by definition takes place into and according to the larger societal (white) model of culture and behavior. Thus, if Negroes are to assimilate, it is they who must give up their black identity and subculture to be comfortably integrated. Many Negroes who seek complete assimilation thus become preoccupied with "proving" to white people that they are "just like all other human beings," i.e. white, and worthy of being assimilated. At the same time they express their willingness to give up all elements of their black identity. This in itself means to them that they are giving up something of inferior or negative value to gain something of greater value: a white identity.

In seeking acceptance among whites many Afro-Americans expend a great deal of internal energy trying to prove that they are all right. But this is a vain and fruitless effort because "personal acceptability" has to be repeatedly proven to each new group of whites. Thus, before a Negro can be an individual he must first prove that he is a human. The Negro groups' vigorous pursuit of middle-class status symbols is frequently an overdetermined attempt to demonstrate to the white man, as well as to themselves, that they can be successful, worthwhile human beings. White America, however, has lumped all Negroes together into one collective group. Hence, there can be no "individual freedom" for any one Negro until there is "group freedom" for all.

That an individual can achieve individual status only through changing his group's status, is, however, an idea foreign to American thought. The Negro, like other Americans, has accepted the belief (descended from the tenets of the Protestant Ethic) that individuals succeed or fail solely as a result of their individual efforts. Thus, an individual's worth is assessed solely on the basis of his merits: he is accepted or rejected because of what he is as an individual. The acceptance by the Negro of this idea of individual merit has worked to his detriment—for it has operated to sustain a delusion in the face of a contradicting reality. It would perhaps be more realistic for black people to develop and orient themselves in terms of a sense of "community" and follow this path as a means of overcoming barriers to them as a group. Only then will acceptance or rejection as *individuals* follow. Achievement of this "group freedom," however, requires undoing racial self-hatred, expending greater group assertiveness for social and political action, and adopting a positive and proud stance toward themselves and others.

Those individuals and organizations who reject the integration philosophy for improving the position of Negroes in American society focus on the achievement of group freedom maintaining that only through strength as a group can black men win human dignity and power. Among these advocates would be those who are committed to the philosophy of "black power" or "black consciousness."

As we mentioned, an important issue in the emancipation of black people is self-determination and fate control. "Black consciousness" movement supporters argue that as long as Negroes are powerless politically and do not have a degree of control over their own communities, they will remain psychological beggars in a white man's house. For instance, they ask, why shouldn't the black community have the final word about the type of policemen that are permitted in their community? Why should a white man downtown be able to send white racist police who shout or think "nigger" into the black community to "enforce the law?" Why, they reason, can't black communities have some degree of autonomy in governing their community, particularly since white controlled urban governments have vested interests in protecting the majority white interests? Who is watching out for black interests? Following the same line of reasoning, black consciousness supporters maintain that local groups should have some say in deciding who will teach in their schools, who will run local welfare departments, in short, who will control their local institutions. To many blacks this does not represent "separatism"; it is simply democracy. The next question, however, is whether or not all-black institutions can provide Negroes with a more stable, positive sense of identity and self-esteem.

It is known that such groups and individuals as the Black Muslims and Malcolm X have frequently had many positive and constructive effects on members of the black community. This group has brought greater self-reliance and dignity to hard-core, untouchable segments of the Negro community. The Muslims were once the one major Negro group (now there are others of the Black Power orientation) that called for separation of the races and black self-sufficiency as an alternative approach to the remedy of the black man's problems of negative identity and self-esteem. Observers generally agree that the Muslims were quite effective in rehabilitating many anti-social and criminal types by fostering in them a positive self-image and pride in their blackness. This group also afforded blacks a channel for expressing their rage at the "white devils." The significant fact is that the Muslims were able to alleviate much of the individual Negro's self-hatred without holding up or espousing integration or "full acceptance" of the black man into American white society.

Other black consciousness groups have instilled pride and esteem in Negroes by emphasizing Negro history and achievements. Programs based on this philosophy can build Negro self-confidence and self-assertion by calling upon black men to think and do for themselves. They may also provide the stimulus for more independent thought and grass-roots problem-solving and lead to the development of community leadership. Such programs seem to have the potential for undoing much of the black man's self-hatred and emasculation and these are the feelings which in part lead to behavior destructive of self and others. Finally, such "race consciousness" programs can constructively channel the Negro frustrations and anger which now lead to destructive violence and riots.

The question must be raised, however, whether "all black" programs will in some ways lead to more identity and self-esteem problems for the Negro since such groups would always exist within a surrounding dominant white culture and would run the risk of being considered inferior. Can you really build a sense of community and pride in the ghettos when these neighborhoods carry the stigma of forced segregation by and from the white community? Can people develop a pride in a neighborhood that is made up of dilapidated housing usually in the most dismal part of our cities? Definitive answers to these questions cannot yet be given. We would suggest, however, that if Negroes were truly *equals* in the larger society, a black subculture could exist much in the same way that America has subcultures of other national and racial groups such as the Jews, Irish, Chinese, etc. That is, if community derives from choice and is among people who feel common bonds, it can be a more salutary situation for blacks than if people of disparate interests, abilities and needs are forced together in a ghetto solely on the basis of a common skin color.

News dispatches make it clear that despite the drive for racial integration, it is being vigorously resisted by the white population, particularly in the area of housing. Therefore, we can expect to have isolated, predominantly black communities for a long time to come. Black Power advocates hold that the potentiality of these communities cannot be ignored while integration is awaited. They insist on building strong black-based institutions now. Whether these can become positive communities founded on common interests and supported by pride—or will stay run-down ghettos that are encampments of human misery—remains to be seen. But the answer rests with both blacks and whites: whether blacks will support this development, and whether whites will allow the movement to proceed without insuperable harassment.

We have discussed in the preceding pages the psychological predispositions which have been generated in the Negro by virtue of his position and relationship in the American social system. We have also given some attention to the consequences of these psychic orientations and the programs and philosophies which have arisen to attempt to change them. It remains for us to suggest what we see as the implications of all this.

Since the black man's need for a sense of self-worth, self-assertion, and independence cannot be met through token integration and since assimilation appears to be a remote possibility, it seems logical that both black and white men must turn to the development and rehabilitation of Negro communities. In this endeavor, however, it is crucial that as much responsibility as possible be placed in the hands of black men since self-development and self-determination lead to a greater sense of self-worth and power.

The white establishment can help to alleviate those problems that afflict black Americans by undoing white supremacy and the oppression of colored peoples. In doing this, white people will have to give up some share of their control and power over black communities. At the same time the white community must earnestly struggle for open housing so that Negroes can have a *free choice* about where they will live. With a choice, the many Negroes who choose to live among blacks will know that they have exercised their free will rather than that they have acquiesced to powers forcing them into a box.

In our cities, white officials can help to build the status of black communities by making them centers of business and cultural attraction for *all* the people. Why not have major theaters, museums, trade centers, located in black communities as part of a general rehabilitation program for the ghettos? There are many other small ways in which the black ghettos could be made part of the mainstream of our urban centers. Even though much has been said in the past decades about the urgent need for jobs, decent housing, and quality education and training programs, very little has been done to implement these ideas. The society is now paying with urban disorder and riots for this chronic neglect in alleviating some of these basic problems. The availability of jobs is especially crucial for the black man in his struggle for dignity. Not only do jobs give men a sense of importance and self-worth, they may also be a channel for the appropriate release of aggression. As in sublimation and displacement they may allow black men to express the assertiveness that has been so long dammed up.

It is also obvious that if we are to do something to stabilize the Negro family we must begin by providing secure jobs for the black man. Men without work cannot fulfill their role and responsibility as husbands and fathers. The entire welfare system must be remodeled so that it will encourage the growth and independence of its recipients. These are only a few of the many social and economic programs that can be developed to alleviate these deplorable human conditions.

It becomes obvious after this long discussion of the psychology of a minority group that this is a subject which cuts across broad social, economic, and political areas. The subject and its implications for social change cannot be considered in isolation. In order to relieve the psychic problems of Negroes which presently manifest themselves in self-hatred, suppressed aggression, non-assertiveness, and dependence, we must address ourselves to the many ramifications of white racism in America.

The President's Commission on Civil Disorders has already made important recommendations for taking a decisive step in solving some of these problems. However, this arduous task requires the creative minds, brave spirits, and imaginative plans of all Americans who are sincerely concerned with the future of this country.

BIBLIOGRAPHY

1. KATZ, I., and L. BENJAMIN. Effects of White Authoritarianism in Biracial Work Groups, *J. Abnormal and Soc. Psych.*, 61:448. 1960.

2. PETTIGREW, T. F. *A Profile of the Negro American.* Princeton: D. Van Nostrand Co., Inc. 1964.

3. GLAZER, N., and D. P. MOYNIHAN. *Beyond the Melting Pot.* Cambridge: MIT Press. 1963.

THE POLITICS OF RACE RELATIONS

CHARLES V. HAMILTON
Roosevelt University

I have been asked to prepare a paper dealing with my views on how the social and political barriers to change in race relations can be bridged. And this paper is to be written within the general context of the theme of the conference: "Short Term and Emergency Measures to Avert Urban Violence."

I suspect that most political scientists who study American politics would conclude that the nature of the American political system is such that it is not particularly suited to rapid or short-term solutions to problems like racial conflict in America. The American political process, it is said, is understandably a slow process. The pluralistic nature of the society makes negotiating, bargaining, and compromising primary means of pursuing one's goals. This may well be true when we focus on certain (or most) kinds of issues put into the political system. But my view is that, that protracted, tedious process—yielding only incremental change in the short-run—is a luxury the society can no longer afford when we begin to talk about race relations. This becomes particularly true when one group feels that it has seldom, if ever, been a legitimate participant in that process.

The issue of race and politics has developed to a point where we must rethink our views about 1) the legitimate ways to raise issues, and 2) some appropriate ways to go about solving those issues.

Quite frankly, I am writing this paper with the background of five years of intense, destructive rebellions in the black, urban ghettos in mind. I suspect that if we had not experienced the explosions in Harlem, Watts, Newark, Detroit, and countless other places, we would probably not be talking today about "emergency measures" to avert urban violence. So, let me proceed from this "crisis" orientation.

I see the political system responding in either (or possibly in each) of three ways:

1) control—repression
2) equitable distribution of goods and services
3) equitable distribution of decision-making power.

I am going to suggest that any "emergency measures" which overlook number three will probably not effectively bridge the social and political barriers to change. Let me deal with each of these responses, with the intent to spend the bulk of my paper on number three.

1) Control

The people at Brandeis University's Lemberg Center for the Study of Violence, under the direction of John P. Spiegel, issued a report based on their study of various cities: Dayton, Akron, San Francisco, Boston, Cleveland, and Pittsburgh. Firstly, they suggest that a communication system be set up whereby "the black community can signal to whites that conditions in the ghetto are approaching a combustion point." My view is that this will help to deal with the explosion once it occurs, but it will do very little to prevent it from occurring. This is so largely because of the rather spontaneous way these revolts start. Contrary to belief in some places, there is not sufficient evidence to conclude that the urban violence is the result of some carefully (or even loosely) planned strategy by outsiders or insiders.

The Brandeis report describes a four-stage process in the development of a riot: 1) the spark—frequently an incident involving the police; 2) confrontation—crowds begin to assemble, rumors spread, spokesmen try to cool the crowds, or mobilize them to take action in the form of a mass march to the police precinct or city hall; 3) "Roman Holiday" —tension mounts, "youths on the streets begin to throw rocks and bottles, break windows and taunt the police. The youths are in a 'carnival mood' and adults usually take little part"; 4) War—widespread violence with adults joining in.

Proper official responses at stages one through three are crucial in averting stage four: not too much or too little control. If the police step back, fail to make arrests and only attempt to contain the violence within a limited area, they will probably not be successful. Neither should the police panic and overestimate the degree of immediate danger they, personally, are subjected to. In the "Roman Holiday" stage, most of the violence is aimed at property, not people, but this is not usually realized by the police. Thus, if the authorities respond "excessively" to the third stage, this will probably lead to stage four and open warfare.

I am not exceptionally or primarily concerned about this entire analysis, because once the spark ignites, it is then simply a matter of mitigating the damage: lives lost, property destroyed, etc. This is important, but not central to my concern here. I am less concerned with averting stage four than I am with averting the entire event.

It is clear that the political system can and will exercise whatever control is necessary to put down the rebellion. Whatever measures are viewed (or misviewed) as necessary will be used: curfews (limited or around the clock), martial law and, ultimately, if the threat is perceived as grave enough, concentration camps. So we need not spend too much time focusing on this aspect. What is clear, however, is that the extent to which the political system must exercise very repressive measures, to that extent it will be in the process of transforming itself into what many black people think it is already, namely, an authoritarian police state. The repercussions of this in terms of overall repression of civil liberties for all the citizens will be substantial. My point, obviously, is that the first response of control and repression ultimately will only aggravate the problems, not alleviate them. Only temporary cessation of looting, burning, and sniping is achieved, nothing more.

It is quite possible that in the process of imposing severe control measures and setting up a Johannesburg-type state, the larger society will be perfectly willing to live with this as the lesser of other evils. This, of course, is a judgment that would have to be made.

Some may view this as necessary to "restore law and order," but this becomes a rather meaningless response. In terms of imposing control to "restore law and order," what has to be understood is that those persons doing the rioting and those calling for "law and order" are absolutely not in tune with each other. "Law and order" is seen by many in the ghettos as a clear means of perpetuating the existing situation. It was that law that winked at absentee slumlords who violated building codes and failed to repair their buildings. It was that law that participated in the organized crime and prostitution in the ghettos—or, at least, a large number of people think so. Therefore, for the rioter to respond to a call to restore law and order, implies or assumes that he has a respect for it, or even perceives a value to him for doing so. Statements issued in the midst of riots by prestigious persons "calling for an end to violence" may well protect the particular leaders' relationships to various decision-makers. But such statements are meaningless in terms of clarifying issues or getting at the root of the problems. In addition, those doing the rioting really do not read or know about such pronouncements.

We simply can no longer assume that we have a consensual society. The values of the larger society—many of them—simply are not shared by many black people in the ghettos. The value of work and achievement is an example. There is the strong notion in the larger society that if one works hard, one is likely to achieve. And if achievement does not come, it is looked upon as an individual fault of the particular person. Dr. Percy Julian, the Negro chemist, has stated: "The false concept of basic Negro inferiority is one of the curses that still lingers. It is a problem created by the white man. Our children just no longer are going to accept the patience we were taught by our generation. We were taught a pretty little lie—excel and the whole world lies open before you. *I obeyed the injunction and found it to be wishful thinking.*" Rioters in the ghettos are not as articulate as Dr. Julian, but they are just as sensitive. And, thus, they know that they cannot afford the luxury of believing in this system. The incremental, peripheral changes—in statutes, jobs, etc.—are entirely too incremental and too peripheral to make an impact on their growing alienation.

I think I understand why it is difficult for a white American to understand and come to terms with the alienation in the ghettos. Professors Killian and Grigg, in their book, *Racial Crisis in America*, have stated:

. . . most white Americans, even those white leaders who attempt to communicate and cooperate with their Negro counterparts, do not see racial inequality in the same way that the Negro does. The white person, no matter how liberal he may be, exists in the cocoon of a white-dominated society. Living in a white residential area, sending his children to white schools, moving in exclusively white social circles, he must exert a special effort to expose himself to the actual conditions under which large numbers of Negroes live. Even when such exposure occurs, his perception is likely to be superficial and distorted. The substandard house may be overshadowed in his eyes by the television aerial or the automobile outside the house. Even more important, he does not perceive the subjective inequalities inherent in the system of segregation because he does not experience them daily as a Negro does. Simply stated, the white American lives almost all of his life in a white world. The Negro American lives a part of his life in a white world also, but in a world in which he is stigmatized.

So most blacks and most whites come to view life differently in this country. The latter can see no real reason or rationale for rioting and for disturbing law and order and, therefore, the latter are willing to sanction control in its most repressive form. The former can perceive rioting as a very meaningful way to draw attention to an intolerable situation or simply to hurt an insensitive system, even if the harm—as it obviously is —is reciprocal, and overly so. And when control in its most repressive form is imposed, it is seen as a measure to perpetuate the conditions of institutional racism.

2) *Equitable distribution of goods and services*

Once the violence erupts, it *will* be put down. Then, invariably, public and private spokesmen begin to make statements, appoint committees, hold meetings, issue reports which usually end up saying that there must be more jobs, more and better housing, better schools, perhaps even better transportation facilities, etc., for the residents in the ghettos. In other words, something must be done to share more equitably the goods and services of the society with the under-class. This is carefully phrased so as not to appear to be "rewarding" violence, but everyone understands that the heightened concern is a direct result of the violent explosions. We can, as a society, phrase it any way we like to protect our own egos and/or our own conception of legitimate ways issues get raised and resolved in this society. But I think it is clear that until the cities started blowing up and burning down there was only minimal concern or minimal effort to deal with the problems. Or to state it differently: there was general belief that "progress was being made," and general belief that there was rather broad acceptance of the path and pace of that progress among black citizens.

Surely, there have to be more jobs, more and better houses, etc. There should be no argument on this point, and since there are several other papers speaking to these aspects, I will move to my third point.

3) *Equitable distribution of decision-making power*

This is the core of my paper. I think that if we concentrate simply on numbers one and two, we will be missing the boat. I firmly believe that it is no longer (if ever it was) sufficient to give people only material, economic things, and I would especially suggest that this is the case with black people in this country at this time. I am fully aware of views contrary to mine. Writing in the October 21, 1967, issue of *The New Republic* in an article entitled: "Limits of the New Left," Christopher Jencks said: "If . . . you ask poor people what is wrong with America, they will usually complain about the *results* of decisions which affect their lives, not the *process* by which the decisions are made. They want good schools or good housing; relatively few of them want a voice in the operation of these facilities if the results are satisfactory."

I think this is not entirely correct. The soundings we get from many segments of the black community tell another story. The most important and significant thing that came out of Governor Romney's 19-day tour of the nation's ghettos was not his discovery of and amazement at the widespread discontent and bitterness and hatred, but a statement made to him on the West Side of Chicago. The statement was buried deep in a news story in the *Chicago Sun-Times* (September 21, 1967): "Half a dozen young black-power militants told him, 'We don't want your houses. We want to be equal.'" It is crucial to understand the implications of such a statement. Those young people were saying that it was not enough simply to deal in equitable distribution of goods and services; there must be an equitable distribution of decision-making power. I am suggesting that vast masses of people do not want to be mere *recipients* of the system, but they are clamoring to be *participants* in the decision-making processes of that system.

I do not intend to advocate some notion of the "cult of the poor," or champion what I call "local peopleitis." I very strongly intend to argue that the society has to take into account the idea that people somehow must be made to feel a part of the society. My idea of a legitimate political system involves the feeling among citizens that they have a personal stake in what is going on. People do not blow up or burn down what they feel they are a legitimate part of.

Mr. Jencks said that most people do not want a voice in the operation of things "if the results are satisfactory." This is an important "if." Already, there has set in a pervasive alienation, a distrust, a lack of confidence in the self-rectifying ability of the system. Many of the goods and services that are and will be given will be viewed as a continuation of the welfare-colonial system. Whether we believe it or not, they will be viewed as reluctant dole exacted at the cost of threat perceived in terms of violence. And there is the clear understanding that what the reluctant donor giveth, he can (and probably will) taketh away.

We can concentrate our efforts on programs aimed at how much money we can spend and how fast we can spend it. We can devise public and private ways to build new houses, new schools, and new recreational areas. But if we just donate these things (something like the percolating theory of wealth), I am suggesting we will find that those same beneficiaries, who are still excluded, will take those goods and services and still blow up the cities. And they will do so precisely because they have not really been included in—where the decisions about housing, schools, recreational areas, etc., are made. (In a moment I will describe a suggestion made recently to the Chicago Board of Education which runs directly counter to my suggestion.) They will do so, because they will feel that these things are only the result of a paternalistic, larger society acting out of a perceived threat to its self-interest. I think they are correct in that feeling. Therefore, in order to legitimize the distribution of goods and services, it becomes crucial to have the black recipients in a position where they can speak for and protect *their* self-interest without having to resort to violence to do so. It is important to understand that large numbers of blacks believe that if the threat of violence is removed, there will be a slackening of interest on the part of the decision-makers. There is the belief that white Americans are going to do only as much as they absolutely have to do any way. We must not forget that most interesting editorial in the *Saturday Evening Post* of September 10, 1966:

We are all, let us face it, Mississippians. We all fervently wish that the Negro problem did not exist, or that, if it must exist, it could be ignored. Confronted with the howling need for decent schools, jobs, housing, and all the other minimum rights of the American system, we will do our best, in a half-hearted way, to correct old wrongs. The hand may be extended grudgingly and patronizingly, but anyone who rejects that hand rejects his own best interests. For minimum rights are the only rights that we are willing to guarantee, and above those minimum rights there is and will continue to be a vast area of discrimination and inequity and unfairness, the area in which we claim the most basic right of all—the right to be stupid and prejudiced, the right to make mistakes, the right to be less and worse than we pretend, the right to be ourselves.

If we want to focus on short-term and emergency measures to avert urban violence, then I would strongly suggest that we talk about legitimate ways to involve people.

In the field of housing and urban renewal, we must learn to routinely consult and listen to local community groups about what type of structures to build, who is to build them, where they are to be built.

In public education, it is important to encourage more community-parent participation in and control over the local schools, after the fashion of I.S. 201 in Harlem, or the Ocean Hill Brownsville district in

Brooklyn, or the Adams-Morgan School District in Washington, D.C.
I would strongly urge that the mentality evidenced by the consultants'
recommendations to the Chicago Board of Education dealing with the
decision to impose busing on black parents be rejected. The report (re-
ferred to as the Redmond Report) clearly states on page B-20:

> The assignment of students outside their neighborhood may be objected to by
> Negro parents who prefer that their children attend the segregated neighbor-
> hood school. This viewpoint cannot be ignored. Prior to implementation of
> such a transfer policy the administration must take steps to reassure apprehen-
> sive sending area parents that transfer will be beneficial not only in terms of
> integration but of improved education for their children. The generation of a
> favorable consensus in the designated sending area is important. If such a con-
> sensus is unobtainable, the transfer program would have to proceed without
> a popular base. In the light of the dismal alternatives such a program perhaps
> should proceed even without consensus, but every effort should be made to
> attain it.

If we continue in this blatant disregard for the wishes and desires of
people, then those plans deserve to fail. One sure way to guarantee continued violence is to perpetuate the kind of thinking illustrated in the
above paragraph.

My data from talking to people in many different ghetto circumstances
reveal clearly to me that what masses of people want and perceive to be
more important is more involvement in the schools, and increased quality. If we start to bus black children all over the city, this will operate
against parental participation, because parents will not be able, in many
instances, to travel long distances to school meetings. In addition, it is
reasonable to assume that many of those parents will not feel comfort-
able in school meetings in strange communities and among people probably more adept at committee-managing than themselves. The black
parents will be absorbed (and controlled) again in a sea of whiteness.
Likewise, we should learn from the experiences of the directors of some
Urban Progress Centers in this city. One director has stated that it is
virtually impossible to get large numbers of black youths to go individ-
ually to apply for a job in the white community. They feel isolated and
surrounded by a hostile world. Only when large numbers of them are
sent, do they feel secure . . . a security based on numbers and being with
their kind. Therefore, Mr. James Griggs of the poverty program in Chicago has stated that his particular agency has concluded that the best way
to build confidence among the black people is to engage them first in

activities in their own neighborhoods. I would suggest that the same formula should be applied to community-school matters.

We must begin to create conditions which will *facilitate* participation, not make it more difficult. This is especially crucial if we begin to take a more comprehensive, family-oriented view toward education (which I think is essential), rather than a narrow view which focuses merely on the child. Quality education in the ghetto means to me new ways of involving the total family in the educational process—in their immediate environment. It means local, community-oriented schools relating to the family in and out of a structured classroom situation for 10 to 12 hours per day. This involves everyone from pre-school through to the parents, discussing curriculums, schedules, etc., with them. It means building total family recreational programs around the community schools, and, also, having as many job situations develop out of this situation as possible. I am not merely talking about some traditional adult education program in the evening and hiring a few mothers per week for child care or as teacher-aides. I am suggesting a much more family-school integrated program. The school could become the center of life, not just from 9:00 A.M. to 3:00 P.M., September to June, with time off for good behavior. It could become a year-round affair. And if we include people *in* on the vital decision-making processes, we will then begin to see dividends of the kind we are interested in.

I am fully aware that this is rather unheard of in mass, complex, industrialized societies where many people would prefer and tend to opt for nightly television. But *something* is wrong with the character of life in our cities for vast masses of people. Structural *exclusion* and perpetuating the welfare-handout system will not get at it. The challenge of our time is not how much money we can or cannot spend, but how can we set about to activate masses of previously unengaged people.

I am aware that this view challenges our conception of expertise and "qualification." I am also aware that we probably should rethink our criteria for judging people "qualified." I am reminded of the statement made by the *vice-president of the Philadelphia school board*, Rev. Henry Nichols: 75 per cent of the black students graduated from Philadelphia high schools in June, 1967, were "functionally illiterate." He stated that this was due, in large measure, to the fact that the school system in that city simply did not know how to relate to ghetto children. Thus, I am saying that we must stop assuming that certain kinds of people are relevant and qualified simply because they have a string of degrees or other credentials behind their names.

I have not focused on electoral politics in this paper, because I do not see the electoral process—except possibly in a very few isolated places—as yielding the kinds of short-term, emergency returns we are talking about. Exceptions might be in those places like Gary and Cleveland where black people have worked hard to elect black candidates. These victories, which are simply first steps, might serve to bolster the confidence of large numbers of black people that they can achieve meaningful results through the protracted process of electoral politics. This is the short-term result. It remains to be seen how these black mayors of their respective cities can operate effectively to help provide a meaningful life for the citizens.

There is an additional very real and rather immediate result to be realized from my emphasis on immediate involvement of people. We are certainly aware that most of these problems cannot be resolved expeditiously. But, by involving people in the decision-making processes, I would suggest that they would thereby become more sympathetic to the many difficulties involved in resolutions, and would be more prone to accept the protracted nature of resolution. As it stands now, failure to act quickly is perceived (as, indeed, it might be if we look back at that *Saturday Evening Post* editorial) as a desire to procrastinate and maintain the status quo. This stems from and reflects the alienation, the lack of trust, the suspicion.

Another result stems from what we know about the decrease in crime in those areas where there has been concerted, constructive civil rights activity. We have data on this from the Montgomery bus boycott period, also from the civil rights demonstrations in Albany, Georgia, in 1961 and 1962. Some people have suggested that they observed evidence of this in the recent Stokes campaign in Cleveland. Where masses of people become involved in a way meaningful to them, they take pride in themselves and in their communities. They, in a sense, police themselves. Not only is there less time and energy for acts of crime, but people come to see the violence as dysfunctional to *their* overall program. They can replace the violence with significant, personal activity calculated in their own terms. This is far better than meaningless, pious pronouncements made once the violence erupts.

Perhaps this sounds like a tactic to co-opt people into an attitude of patience. I do not prefer to debate this. We can agree, however, that the cities are blowing up, lives are being lost. And if what I am suggesting turns out to be just another gimmick to delay, to pacify people, then it will quickly be seen as such, and the fires will start all over again, and the troops will have to be called out again.

I would hope that my emphasis on a genuine equitable distribution of decision-making power would be seen as a sincere way to avert or, at least, to mitigate further events of violence. We could be imaginative and collectively creative about all aspects of ghetto life: housing, schools, jobs, law enforcement, health, welfare, recreation.

I am not unaware of the immense political problems involved in such suggestions. But in the final analysis, I can only hope that the larger society would see its self-interest tied into these solutions and move to protect that self-interest in meaningful, constructive ways, not simply in terms of control measures.

I would strongly suggest that we encourage local, community groups to begin working on what I call "internal ghetto goals": absentee slumlords, exploitative merchants and loan sharks, inadequate ghetto schools. These are "bread and butter" issues around which sizable numbers of people can be organized. And with substantial help from officials, they can realize rather immediate, visible victories. Some of the most effective and astute organizers in the black communities—the local black minister —will tell us that a major principle of community organization in their indigenous areas centers on giving the people quick, visible victories. All the time they are involved, not in some superficial, OEO-type of "maximum feasible participation" way (as it is practiced in many cities). Then the people will begin to develop a *habit* of organization, a *consciousness* of ability to exert power—things Harold Laski correctly said they lack.

We should encourage (as was done in the Chelsea district of New York City in the summer, 1966) teen-age youths to study the municipal building codes and then proceed to check violations in their communities. I saw this program work there, and the immediate dividends were substantial. The youths—some of whom were former or present gang leaders and members—learned how to organize, how to make demands on the building inspectors, and how to follow up. If direct action (picketing, etc.) was necessary, they would take it. Remedial educational classes (frequently with the complicated municipal codes as texts) were held in the morning, and they would go out into the "field" in the afternoon—

pencil and clipboard in hand. These youths were involved. They felt relevant for the first time, and they took a new pride in themselves and in their communities.

Granted, neither this nor the comprehensive integrated-family-education idea will solve all the problems. There are many problems "external" to the ghetto (jobs, more housing, for example) which inevitably will involve clashes with the white communities. But no one assumed (or should have at any rate) that we would come here with panaceas.

While we may understand, we should all be disturbed by the tone and language of President Johnson on Friday, November 3, 1967, at the swearing in of the new government of Washington, D.C. He hit hard on the issue of control of domestic disorders and crime. "The time has come, in my judgment, when the American people are going to rise up and revolt against the lawbreaker in this country," he said. "We are going to have to obey the law." ". . . So if you need twice as many policemen, if you need to pay them twice as much, if you need twice as much communication, if you need extra automobiles and motor vehicles and educated people, then let's start to work to get them. But let's clean up crime here."

I think this language is very short-sighted. It is not the kind of language—partisan political considerations aside—I prefer to hear from my public officials who should be taking every opportunity to think and articulate creatively. More policemen, with higher salaries, and more police cars with advanced radio systems are not our long-term or short-term solutions. Public officials, with immense political influence, should not mislead the public in that manner. If they do, they only pave the way for "the fire next time." Our responsibility to the total society is much greater than that, precisely because the problems are not that simple.

I think it is important to keep in mind what Professor C. E. Black stated in his book, *The Dynamics of Modernization*: ". . . This is the first time in world history that peoples of such disparate backgrounds have sought to solve the problem of living together in an advanced society." On the subject of violence, he wrote: "Violence or at least the threat of violence is inherent in all political relations, but in modern times it has become endemic. To say this is not to justify or to advocate violence. It is merely to note the fact that violence—as is the case with other forms of social disorganization—has become increasingly common in modern times. People tend to cling tightly to the traditional way of doing things, identifying their personal security with the culture with which they were indoctrinated in childhood, and the scale of violence can be reduced only when, under firm leadership, people become convinced that change is necessary."

A president of the United States should be spending his time and resources preparing the society for such necessity. He has no more urgent task.

Let us not focus on how sophisticated we can become in control measures, or *merely* on equitable distribution of goods and services (thereby further institutionalizing a recipient class), but let us marshal our talents and time to think and implement new ways of equitably distributing decision-making power, and creative ways of involving people. Then, hopefully, we can begin to look forward not to the fire next time, but to a society worth saving.

THE AMERICAN DILEMMA: PERSPECTIVES AND PROPOSALS FOR WHITE AMERICANS

HAROLD W. PFAUTZ
Brown University

It should be self-evident that the long hot summer of 1967 and the cruel spring of 1968 have been in the making for two hundred years; that the collective disorders are not race riots in the usual sense of the term but expressive insurrections, fed by the fires of aggravated frustrations, fueled by the colossal indifference of the majority of affluent dominant whites, and touched off by the growing vacuum of civic leadership and commitment to democratic values on the local community level. The shattering of the domestic tranquillity, which is the bed-rock of any viable social life, attests not to the sickness of Negro Americans so much as it reveals the sickness of American communities. The violent outbursts are neither plots nor programs but indicators of one basic fact—that no community can survive, can be a "community," if literally thousands of its members, if proportions of its population ranging from 5 to over 50 per cent, are literally outside its social system.

Nothing has made this clearer than the Report of the National Advisory Commission on Civil Disorders, the Kerner Commission, a report which was issued on March 1, 1968, and whose recommendations have yet to be taken seriously by white administrators, white legislators, white political leaders anywhere in the nation. What was the Report's basic conclusion but that "Our nation is moving toward two societies, one black, one white—separate and unequal."[1]

It is no longer a question of speaking "for" the Negro but of speaking the truth to white Americans. Myrdal's "an" American dilemma has clearly become "the" American dilemma. With few exceptions the reactions of the country's leadership to date only underscores the validity of the subtitle of his classic, twenty-five-year-old study: *The Negro Problem and Modern Democracy*. In fact, frightened mayors, politicized city councils, and defensive police commissioners—all of whom understandably suffer from a trained incapacity to deal with the kind of crisis we face—hold the future of our democratic polity in their hands. For, lack-

---

[1] *Report of the National Advisory Commission on Civil Disorders* (New York: Bantam Books, Inc., 1968), p. 1.

ing statesmanlike leadership on the local community level, panicky populations may all too easily succumb to the notion that the Public Safety requires increasingly repressive measures and may settle for control as their ultimate value. But what are the truths, and where do they lead us?

In the first place, no prolonged, extensive studies are necessary to arrive at relevant and valid conclusions concerning the congeries of social trends and factors that comprise the long-term causes of the epidemic of urban violence. Indeed, one of the most awe-inspiring aspects of the situation is the seemingly limitless capacity of most white Americans for selective inattention and self-deception in regard to the American dilemma. This is especially shocking in the face of a communications revolution and knowledge explosion that have vividly revealed every decaying nook and corner of the ghetto and put the name and fact of Ellison's "invisible man" on the front pages of our mass periodicals and daily newspapers. And this is not to mention the stream of surveys and studies conducted by social scientists and by education, health, and welfare agencies which have further publicized the scale of the problem and the sorry facts of the Negro American's predicament, nor even the mass sales of the Kerner Commission Report or the attention devoted to it in the media.

In fact, since 1920 the Negro population has doubled, now stands at approximately 20 million, and is predicted approximately to double again by 1990.[2] In fact, by 1970 half of our fifty largest cities (over 100,000 population) will have Negro populations of 25 per cent or more; fourteen of these communities will have Negro populations of 40 per cent or more; and the five largest American cities will have Negro populations of more than 700,000, a number which will be surpassed by the total populations (Negro and white) of only seventeen American communities.[3]

To the sheer demographic scale of the problem must be added the scale and pace of the social trends and cultural drifts that have taken place since World War II. These have resulted not merely in bringing about significant changes in the objective characteristics of the Negro population but have underwritten a social psychological development that is the basis of the contemporary Negro revolt—the rise of a new

[2] U.S. Bureau of the Census, *Current Population Reports*, Series P-25, No. 359, "Projections of the Population of the United States," (February 20, 1967).

[3] *Congressional Quarterly*, August 1966, pp. 1861–1862.

concept of self. Thus, in less than a generation, Negro Americans have been transformed from a regional, rural, and agricultural population to an essentially national, urban, and industrial population. Moreover, formal anti-discriminatory and desegregation policies and practices initiated by government and private agencies at all levels, culminating in the Supreme Court decision of 1954 and the Civil Rights Acts of more recent vintage, have provided Black Americans with a new mirror for self-conception.[4] And, regardless of how little these policies have been put into operation, they have given moral as well as legal sanction to Negro aspirations. Further, a new leadership has developed that is no longer accommodating and beholden for its status to the dominant whites. Consequently, it is no longer confined to the traditional "protest within the status quo." The rise of the new protest groups— C.O.R.E., S.N.C.C., S.C.L.C., and the varieties of Black Nationalism— indicates the degree to which traditional forms of protest—represented by the Urban League and the N.A.A.C.P.—no longer meet the needs of a new generation of Negro Americans. The final result has been the dramatic reversal of the traditional formula of American race relations: whereas as late as 1944 Myrdal found the Negro's life to be primarily a reaction to "primary pressures from the side of the dominant whites," today, black men act and white men react.

The tragic paradox, of course, is that despite these developments, the social and economic situation of the vast majority of Negro Americans has not significantly improved and in some areas has actually deteriorated. No really significant gains have been made in either income or in employment.[5] Today, there is more rather than less residential segregation.[6] School desegregation has proceeded at a snail's pace at best and has involved studied tokenism and adamant and violent resistance at worst.[7]

At this point in time, it is especially important that we should not be misled by the development of a Negro middle class. That a significant

[4] Cf., Harold W. Pfautz, "The New 'New Negro': Emerging American," *Phylon*, 24 (Fourth Quarter, 1963), pp. 360–368.

[5] Cf., Otis Dudley Duncan, "Discrimination Against Negroes," *The Annals of the American Academy of Political and Social Science*, 371 (May, 1967), pp. 85–103.

[6] Cf., Karl E. Taeuber, "Residential Segregation," *Scientific American*, 213 (August, 1965), pp. 12–19.

[7] Cf., U.S. Office of Education, James S. Coleman *et al.*, *Equality of Educational Opportunity* (Washington, D.C.: U.S. Government Printing Office, 1966), p. 3.

number (although very small proportion) of Negro Americans have achieved success in the traditional American terms of education, occupation, and life-style does not and cannot solve the basic fault in the social structures of our nation and its local communities. The myth of opportunity and the possibility of mobility from log cabin to White House can be validated for most white Americans by the factual success of an identifiable few. This does not, however, hold true for the vast mass of Negroes.

Although Franklin Frazier was correct in his bitter critique of the "Black Bourgeoisie" as a society of "status without substance," he failed to generalize the meaning of his hypothesis.[8] It is not just that the "Black Bourgeoisie" is unreal but that the concept of a Negro class structure is unreal. In fact, the status of the middle-class Negro is not validated by either the white or the black communities. In the latter, the element of mutual respect (however grudging) that is the basis of any viable status system is conspicuous by its absence: lower-class Negroes are not only jealous but suspicious of the motives of their middle-class fellows; and lower-class Negroes know (or, at least, sense) that despite their success, middle-class blacks still do not really "have it made."[9] The inner and narrowly social barriers of the color line remain unbreached; the successful, middle-class Negro is still, for most white Americans, a Negro and outside the status system of "their" community.[10]

To be sure, Negro Americans seek power. The entire thrust of recent historical and social science research on the Negro in America has been in the direction of the revelation that the ultimate basis of racial minority status lies in the historical uses of power. This is the basic connotation of the contemporary battle cry, "Black Power"—the assumption that racial minority status is a function of politics and

[8] Cf., E. Franklin Frazier, *Black Bourgeoisie* (Glencoe, Ill.: The Free Press, 1958), pp. 195–212.

[9] The Kerner Commission found, for example, that the typical rioter during 1967 was not only "extremely hostile to whites" but that his hostility was more apt to be "a product of social and economic class than of race," and that he was "almost equally hostile toward middle-class Negroes." *Report, op. cit.,* pp. 128–29.

[10] As Blumer has noted in his thoughtful discussion of "the color line" as the central dimension along which the racial problem lies and is formed, it appears as a series of ramparts rather than a single barrier, and its inner reaches lie "outside the formal controls of a society: it is a matter of personal attitude and thus falls inside the area of individual determination." Cf., Herbert Blumer, "The Future of the Color Line," *mimeo,* n.d., p. 18.

history rather than of biology and thus subject to change. Surely, the analogue is "White Power"; for, whatever differences exist are essentially stylistic and these, only of relatively recent vintage. But, power, however fundamental in the functioning of social relationships, is primarily eventful in nature; it is visible only in crises. Under normal conditions, it is accommodated as authority, its forceful qualities are overlaid with the trappings of prestige, and its workings are assimilated in a process of consensual validation.

Viewed in these terms, power is but the proximate aim of the Negro revolution. In the long run, the goal is the goal of all human beings— *status*. I refer here not to status in the narrow sense of prestige but in the broader sense of having a place and function in, of being a member of "the" community. To be a member of the community in the most fundamental sense of the term is to have one's concept of self validated by significant others. To be a member of the community is to be able to cash in one's educational, income, and occupational gains for status. The fact of the matter, however, is that Negro Americans have been in but not of the community. And, the recent disturbances in our cities throughout the country are a vivid illustration of the stark fact that a significant and growing number (especially of the younger generation of Negro Americans) are not so much "alienated" as they are dissociated, for to be alienated implies that one has once been a part of something.

It is also important that we recognize that the various efforts on the part of the federal government to deal with the American dilemma —the Poverty Program, the school desegregation guidelines, and the various commissions concerned with equal employment opportunity— are aimed at the interests involved in what some have called "class politics" in contrast to "status politics."[11] Such interests (e.g., income, occupation, education) are not only subject to mobilization and distribution on the part of a government but "dissent is typically expressed in proposals for reform, tends to be highly programmatic, and is also future-oriented and forward-looking, in the sense that it looks

[11] Cf., Richard Hofstadter, "The Pseudo-Conservative Revolt," in: Daniel Bell (ed.), *The Radical Right* (New York: Doubleday and Co., Inc., 1964), pp. 84–85 and Seymour Martin Lipset, "The Sources of the 'Radical Right,' " in: *ibid.*, pp. 308–309. Hofstadter refers to "*interest politics*, the clash of material aims and needs among various groups and blocs; and *status politics*, the clash of various projective rationalizations arising from status aspirations and other personal motives," Hofstadter, *op. cit.*, p. 84.

to a time when the adoption of this or that program will materially alleviate or eliminate certain discontents."[12]

With the possible exception of some of the peripheral activities of the U.S. Commission on Civil Rights, the interests involved in status politics have been almost completely neglected. Here, of course, "there are no clear-cut solutions . . . there is little or nothing which a government can do."[13] Correlatively, political movements spawned by status anxieties and frustrations typically exhibit irrational motifs. To be sure, the interests involved in status cannot be mobilized and allocated by a government, but this is only to say that status must be carved out in the concrete social process of the local community.

Thus, as the Kerner Commission recommended, the federal government has crucial functions to perform in the articulation of public policy and in the provision of material resources. Massive subsidies are obviously needed in the areas of housing, education, and income. But, it is not just that the government has made too feeble an effort, as Moynihan and others in their affection for the level of abstraction represented by "the Great Society" would have it. Moreover, we should not be led astray by the illusions federal programs present of serving the status interest of Negro Americans; for, they involve only the *ad hoc* institutionalization of status outside the community—much like finding a niche for the mental patient by giving him a job in the asylum. Rather, insofar as the private and informal sectors of local communities are not involved in such a manner as to make a place, especially a social place, for Negro Americans inside the going community, federal programs aimed at class interests risk functioning as modes of incitement and lead to a revolution not of rising expectations but of rising frustrations, the fruits of which are visibly more violent and difficult to control.[14]

In this respect, it is important to note that the Kerner Commission, while recommending massive public and private financed programs, proposed three primary objectives for national action to fulfill "our pledge of equality":

[12] *Ibid.*, p. 85.

[13] Lipset, *op. cit.*, p. 309.

[14] In a recent communication to the author, Professor Everett Hughes of Brandeis University recalled Robert E. Park's observation that a Chinese "could get wealthy and powerful in Hawaii, but he had only position, not status."

—Opening up all opportunities to those who are restricted by racial segregation and discrimination, and eliminating barriers to their choice of jobs, education, and housing.

—Removing the frustration of powerlessness among the disadvantaged by providing the means for them to deal with the problems that affect their own lives, and by increasing the capacity of our public and private institutions to respond to these problems.

—Increasing communications across racial lines to destroy stereotypes, to halt polarization, to end distrust and hostility, and to create common ground for efforts toward common goals of public order and social justice.[15]

While none of the above objectives are separable, I would contend that the second is the pivotal one on which the other two depend and is the key to the Commission's goal of the "affirmation of common possibilities, for all, within a single society."

The real and ultimate locus of the American dilemma is not the "Great Society" but the local community: here the heritage of prejudice and discrimination has its concrete and massive debilitating impact on the lives of individuals; here have been the barriers to full participation; here is the locus of the battle and the barricades; and here, finally, is the primary locus of status and self.

Of course, it is not "the community" but white Americans, especially their leaders who, in failing their Negro fellow-citizens, have failed themselves and their democratic society. On the one hand, the callous indifference of middle-class whites is revealed by their headlong physical flight to the suburbs which has made possible their privatized escape from involvement in the problems of the city that is the source of their affluence. Between 1950 and 1960, for example, the white population of New York City decreased by almost one-half million, and the story was the same in Chicago, which experienced a loss of 400,000 whites.[16] The exodus continues: in 1966, 25,000 white students disappeared from the rolls of the public schools of New York City.[17]

On the other hand local community officials, as well as citizens who

[15] Report, op. cit., p. 413.

[16] Cf., Warren S. Thompson and David T. Lewis, Population Problems (New York: McGraw-Hill, Inc., 1965), p. 167.

[17] New York Times, June 7, 1966, p. 1.

play important roles in the informal power structure, have, more often than not, conducted their business as usual, in the manner of a "white Bourgeoisie." They have failed utterly to define the situation in such a manner as would enlist the energies and competencies of their constituents not only to understand the nature and urgency of the American dilemma but also to act productively in the service of its amelioration.

The failure of local community leadership is explained in part by the fact that the mayors of many of our cities as well as the citizens who serve on the policy-making boards of municipal agencies comprise a social generation whose conceptions and preconceptions of Negroes were formed from 30 to 50 years ago. Until recently, these have been under no real pressure to change and, unfortunately, many have been hardened by the riotous run of events. Nor is it simply that the American city historically has been the cockpit of politics. Rather in recent years, this concept has been wedded to that of "city management." This newer tradition has, perhaps, been most obviously and dysfunctionally expressed in the operations of local urban redevelopment and renewal agencies which, as Kaplan discovered in Newark, N.J., in 1961, "have achieved widespread purposive innovation only at the cost of major democratic values."[18] While honest and competent city management may yield lower tax rates, large-scale physical renewal, economic development, and even, on occasion "the city beautiful," it just as surely precludes responsive and democratic civic leadership. The result is rather a trained incapacity to deal with the type of civic crisis that the revolution in race relations presents.

As late as 1962, for example, the mayor of one New England city could respond to a request for the establishment of a local Human Relations Commission with the revealing observation that he did "not consider it the normal function of municipal government to initiate and promote advanced legislation in the social field." And he went on to say: "In broad terms the function of municipal administration [sic] is to conduct the 'housekeeping' services, protect persons and property, and to enforce the established law." Much of his administration was devoted to the promotion of a massive urban renewal program, the virtues of which were touted nationally by both

---

[18] Harold Kaplan, "Urban Renewal in Newark, New Jersey, The Power Structure of a 'Successful' Program," paper delivered at the 1961 Annual Meeting of the Political Science Association, St. Louis, Missouri, September 6–9, 1961. *Mimeo*, p. 16.

local and federal officials. Unfortunately, it also "succeeded" in forcing the relocation of approximately 80 per cent of the local Negro population in an obvious climate of community prejudice and discrimination, in increasing the amount of residential segregation, and in worsening significantly local race relations.

His younger and recent successor has continued in this tradition. Reelected for a second term, his inaugural address failed even to mention the plight of the city's Negroes but played up physical improvement, fiscal responsibility, and the preservation of order by the police. During the past year, the "new" mayor distinguished himself by a bald (but bootless) attempt to obtain a Model Cities grant without even the formality of a Citizen's Subcommittee on Minority Group Housing as one of the minimal prerequisites for a federal "workable program"; by giving only grudging support and, at critical junctures, even negative leadership to plans to desegregate the public elementary schools; and hardly a week before the city fell victim to the current epidemic of ghetto violence, when chided by the Negro Director of the city Human Relations Committee for the mayor's failure to discuss summer plans for slum areas, by retorting publicly that he was under no obligation to consult with city agencies on such matters. Unfortunately, this sorry history of the failure of civic leadership can be repeated in scores of communities throughout the nation.

If the real locus of the American dilemma is in our local communities, then both formal and informal civic leadership must be developed and engaged to make Negro Americans not only a part of the polity but of the status system as well. In the former case, given the trend to civic management, the most obvious and promising line of attack involves those local community institutions and agencies the policies and operations of which most directly (and, typically, abrasively) bear on the daily nature and course of race relations: the police, the schools, housing authorities, municipal services, city planning and redevelopment agencies. Indeed, precisely in these areas have tokenism or indifference been the typical responses to the legitimate demands of Negro Americans for representation of their interests in policy and practice. Lacking access to these crucial institutions, Black Power has spilled over into the streets.[19]

[19] Significantly, the recent episodes of collective violence have the same pre-political flavor and background that informed the rural and urban riots that took place in France and England during the eighteenth and early nineteenth centuries. The looting and burning are ori-

It is a truism, for example, that one major factor in the kind of race relations a community has is the operating politics of its police department. All too often, as events have clearly demonstrated, the record has been an execrable one. Thus, the Report of the National Advisory Commission on Civil Disorders found that of the twelve deeply held grievances of urban Negroes, "police practices" were ranked first among those in the highest level of intensity.[20] Further, a recently published study of the police department of a West Coast city found that while the police enjoyed an enviable public support in the dominant white community, regardless of class positions, Negroes were almost uniformly critical of the state of police-community relations. Significantly, the issue was not "physical brutality" but abiding attitude as expressed in language, gesture, and approach.

All this, however, is less the fault of the police than another illustration of the lack of concern on the part of the dominant white citizens in American local communities. It is they who have mindlessly allowed their own prejudiced attitudes to be reflected by the police in the daily performance of the latter's "duties"; and it is they who must insist that the public policy be drastically changed in this salient institution. Parenthetically, the current spectacle of policemen and police chiefs making policy pronouncements further suggests the dangerous vacuum that has developed in civic leadership as well as the extent to which the police department has become the most isolated of community agencies.

The situation is much the same in the case of highly politicized school boards, nervous and bureaucratized school administrators, and professionalized city planners. Lacking sensitive, imaginative, courageous, and responsible leadership, fundamentally political and human issues are often transformed into administrative problems, the solutions to which are sought within a narrow range of objective, physical, economic, and technical criteria of "success." To be sure, it has become fashionable to give lip service to human values in the policy statements of these crucial agencies of community life, but their actual operations delude no one, least of all Negro Americans.

---

ented to the same concepts of "a rough, natural justice" that pervaded these earlier forms of protest. Cf., George Rudé, The Crowd in History, 1730–1848 (New York: John Wiley & Sons, Inc., 1964).

[20] Report, op. cit., p. 7.

No complicated programs or lengthy studies are needed here—only the pronouncements of and commitment to operating policies on the part of civic leaders that will guarantee the representation of the in· terests of Negro Americans and that will serve to validate rather than to destroy their self-conceptions as members of the community. Indeed, it is my conviction that precisely here modern social science theory and research have something useful and relevant to say to those who are concerned with the control of events, especially of intergroup hostility and conflict, in institutional contexts. Of course, there has ever been a dysfunctional hiatus between social theory and social practice, if only because social theorists and social practitioners have usually had their careers in different institutional contexts. And, it obviously takes a social disaster of considerable proportions to bring them together, as we are assembled here. Therefore, even at the risk of being pedantic, I would like to take this opportunity to summarize what I believe we have learned. Further, in this I will draw heavily on what I regard to be (and what is probably familiar to you as) the most creative evaluation of research and its implications for practice in the field of race relations ever accomplished—that by the late William C. Bradbury.[21]

Research in race relations has, traditionally, focused on the subjective aspect of the problem—prejudice, viewed as attitude—and regarded this dimension as the independent variable determining the objective aspect of the problem—discrimination, a matter of acts. In these terms, two types of theories have emerged: The first, which Bradbury terms "psychological," sees prejudice as an essentially irrational phenomenon, rooted in the psychic structure of the individual, and discrimination as a compulsive act.[22] The second, which I shall term "cultural," views prejudicial attitudes as essentially non-rational in nature, rooted in the folkways and mores of a society and learned in the context of the child's early socialization experiences in the family, the play group, and from authority figures.[23] Discrimination is seen as custom in the group and as mindless habit in the individual.

[21] William C. Bradbury, "Evaluation of Research in Race Relations," *Inventory of Research in Racial and Cultural Relations*, 5 (Winter-Spring 1953), pp. 99–133.

[22] Cf., e.g., Bruno Bettelheim and Morris Janowitz, "Ethnic Tolerance: A Function of Social and Personal Control," *American Journal of Sociology*, LV (September, 1949), pp. 137–145.

[23] Cf., e.g., Mary Ellen Goodman, *Race Awareness in Young Children* (Cambridge: Addison-Wesley Press, Inc., 1952).

Regardless of the validity of these theoretical perspectives, Bradbury pointed out that they had little strategic relevance as far as control is concerned.[24] Neither a therapeutic assault on individual psyches nor the manipulation of the informally organized social settings of childhood are promising avenues for bringing about change.

Increasingly, however, research in race relations has focused on discrimination—acts, rather than prejudice—attitudes. And this has led to a third type of theory which I shall call "sociological."[25] This, in effect, denies a one-to-one, determinant relationship between private prejudices and individual acts but rather emphasizes the rational, self-conscious character of human conduct and its determination by specific group norms in organized social contexts.[26] Lohman and Reitzes have been especially concerned to state the implications of this view for race relations in contemporary society:

. . . in modern mass society individual behavior is increasingly controlled by deliberately organized collectivities. As concerns home ownership, wages and working conditions, and commercial transactions, the individual's racial attitudes are subordinated to and mobilized by definitions of the situations supplied by organizations.[27]

All of this is simply to say that giant strides in the control and change of individual behavior in the area of race relations can be accomplished in institutional contexts, so long as topside policy is clear and vigorously pursued at all levels. This does not mean, of course, that private prejudices will disappear or that individual conduct in other contexts will not involve discriminatory acts. It does mean, however, that if there is courageous administrative leadership, individual attitudes do not constitute an insuperable barrier to instituting behavioral change.

[24] Bradbury recalls Robin Williams' insight that "the factors which are most important in producing hostility and conflict are by no means the same as those which are most important for control purposes." Bradbury, op. cit., pp. 105–106.

[25] Bradbury speaks of "the economistic hypothesis" which sees discrimination as "merely a more or less rational mode of adaption to the social environment in the course of the pursuit of interests." Ibid., p. 121.

[26] Cf., e.g., Lewis M. Killian, "The Effects of Southern White Workers on Race Relations in Northern Plants," American Sociological Review, 17 (June, 1952); Herbert Blumer, "Social Science and the Desegregation Process," Annals 304 (March, 1956), pp. 137–143; Dietrich C. Reitzes, "Institutional Structure and Race Relations," Phylon 20 (1959), pp. 48–66.

[27] Joseph D. Lohman and Dietrich C. Reitzes, "Note on Race Relations in Mass Society," American Journal of Sociology LVIII (November, 1952), p. 240.

Moreover, the evidence suggests that there is something of a feed-back process at work in the sense that changes in conduct and the correlative experiences that accompany them have an impact on prejudiced attitudes. As Bradbury observed in connection with such policy changes instituted in a government agency:

...once the trend toward merit hiring, merit placement, and merit promotion got rolling, it became a chain reaction, producing its own fuel and advancing at an accelerating pace through its effects upon value-attitudes, beliefs, and interests on both sides of the fading color line and upon the overall distribution of authority and power in the agency and its subunits... Anti-Negro beliefs about racial characteristics affecting the work situation and about the dire consequences of attempting fair employment turned out, with occasional very minor exceptions, to be false. Moreover, they ceased to be believed; they *withered away*.[28]

In both the short and long runs, I propose that the crucial municipal agencies that I have mentioned should embark not only on administrative policies which are self-consciously non-discriminating but, even more important, should constantly measure their goals and means against the vital interests of Negro Americans which, today, are clearly the vital interests of all Americans. Thus, as Otis Dudley Duncan has recently observed, the long-range goal of public policy in every community must be the eradication of the ghetto because it involves restriction of movement, which is a basic threat to the viability of any living organism:

What is intolerable about the ghetto is not merely that housing is old, over-crowded, and vermin-infested—although all of these things are true, and could be remedied if there were a will to do so. What is intolerable is that there is a ghetto at all, except as it might arise from the process of people making unfettered choices as to where they will live. As long as it is known that everyone who is black must live only in certain quarters and must stay away from others, then everyone who lives there—whether or not he would choose to move, given the choice—must day by day and minute by minute experience the restriction and humiliation that this abridgement of freedom implies.[29]

Correlatively, every operating policy not only should be directed to this end but also should in no way assume or support the pattern of segregated living.

[28] Bradbury, *op. cit.*, p. 124.
[29] Otis Dudley Duncan, "After the Riots," *Mimeo*, July 27, 1967.

Parenthetically, it also seems to me that it would be extremely useful and practicable to identify and to recruit as local agency consultants the new grassroots leadership that has been thrown up by the urban revolt. I refer here not to those who have visibility as the result of representing some constituency, however real or unreal, but to those who, in the context of community strife, have come out of nowhere, so-to-speak, and played productive roles.

Beyond these steps which are oriented to the integration of Negro Americans into the polity of the community, white Americans, especially the middle class, must find it in themselves to bear some of the burden of social change. Above all, it is they who must validate the status of middle-class Negro Americans. And this involves nothing less than, at long last, the assimilation of the Negro—divesting him completely of his minority status as the categoric object of fear and anxiety, hatred and condescension. In a word, it is to make him a part of the community of status.

White Americans must also, in the difficult months and years to come, understand and sympathize. One of the prices of more contact across the racial line is the certainty that white and Negro Americans increasingly will mutually disappoint one another and talk past one another. But, it would be temerarious to assume, after two hundred years of physical and social separation, that they necessarily and always take the same things for granted. It is not, for example, that Negro Americans have any stake in collective violence. On the other hand, it is more than possible that "law" and "order" simply do not have the rich connotations that they do for the majority of white Americans. To the masses of ghettoized blacks, "law" is more apt to mean harrassment and personal humiliation, and "order" is essentially foreign to life on the margins or outside the society.

White Americans should also understand that much of the contemporary Negro leadership is a movement rather than an organization leadership. Consequently, it is inherently tenuous and shifting; it often involves more charisma than competence; and typically there are no clearly identifiable and constant constituencies or certain chains of command. It will be tragic indeed if the white power structure holds Negro leaders responsible for events over which they have no control.

Finally, white Americans should understand that the separatist mood and thrust of Black Power are precisely aimed at the status interests of Black Americans and correlatively subject to irrational formulations and expressions. Insofar as the American dilemma has become increasingly transparent and the pace of integration efforts still of token proportion, both the rhetoric and the tactics of the movement have understandably come to focus on the development of a black culture and a black society as the contexts for identity and self-realization.

To be sure, the goals of integration and assimilation have all too often had condescending connotations and involved paternalistic modes of operation. As social processes, however, they are inherently and inevitably two-way affairs. No matter how popular the rhetoric of separatism, white liberals should not settle for what white illiberals have always sought for Black Americans: isolation and the ghettoized self and society.

However much assertion is the effective basis of self, power, like skin color, is a vacuum value; however much blacks have been short-changed in the writing of American history, the past, the present, and even more important, the future of Negroes in America is American. Moreover, like it or no, the empirical possibilities of a bi-racial society in the face of the complex functional interdependencies that inform modern urban social systems are objectively minimal. Hopefully, the ultimate function of Black Power will be the revitalization rather than the bifurcation of our culture and society.

The American dilemma is, after all, historical and social in both its causes and its effects. We are engaged in the enormous task not only of trying to make but also to "beat" history. Therefore, the problem does not lend itself to simple, final, or even technical solutions, except in the twisted minds of true believers. Rather, as a human, social problem, we must, together, contend with it. And, as human beings with limited life spans, it is, perhaps, our style of failure which is more important than unreal investments in "success."

More especially, white Americans must develop what Christopher Lasch has recently termed "a sense of injustice and of the indignities and humiliations which they have increasingly allowed themselves to accept as normal, inevitable, proper, and even 'moral.' "[30] In a word,

[30] Christopher Lasch, *The Decline of Dissent, Katellagete* (Winter, 1966–67), p. 17.

the American dilemma, like war, "is too important to be left to the generals." Only as we begin to act out our own personal commitments, to assure that our community institutions will be informed by, rather than give lip service to, our democratic traditions, will our style of failure be such that we can live in communities with our neighbors and ourselves.

PARTICIPANTS

The following are brief biographies of individuals who participated in the working sessions of the conference.

U.S. Representative *Thomas Ludlow Ashley* of Ohio is a member of the House Committee on Banking and Currency and on Merchant Marine and Fisheries. He is a member of the Center's core group on urban problems.

David Birenbaum was Assistant General Counsel for the National Advisory Commission on Civil Disorders.

Walter J. Blum is Professor of Law, The University of Chicago. He specializes in federal taxation, insolvency, and corporate reorganization. Mr. Blum is co-author of *The Uneasy Case for Progressive Taxation* and *Public Law Perspectives on a Private Law Problem: Auto Compensation Plans.* He is a Fellow of the Center for Policy Study.

Jerald C. Brauer is Professor and Dean of the Divinity School, The University of Chicago. An ordained Lutheran minister, he is a scholar in the field of church history and Christian thought. He is the author of several books including *Protestantism in America.* Dean Brauer is a Fellow of the Center for Policy Study.

Charles J. Calitri is Associate Professor of Education and Director for Projects for the Disadvantaged, Hofstra University. He taught for ten years in East Harlem and is the author of articles in the field of education.

Charles U. Daly is Director of the Center for Policy Study and Vice-President of The University of Chicago. Before coming to the University, he served as a special assistant to Presidents John F. Kennedy and Lyndon B. Johnson.

G. Franklin Edwards is Professor in the Department of Sociology and Anthropology, Howard University, and a member of the National Capitol Planning Commission. He is the author of *The Negro Professional Class* and articles on race relations.

Charles V. Hamilton is Professor and Chairman of the Department of Political Science, Roosevelt University. He is the author of the forthcoming *Negro Politics and Political Modernization* and *The Politics of Civil Rights* and the co-author of *Black Power: The Politics of Liberation in America.*

James F. Hoge, Jr., is managing editor of the *Chicago Sun-Times* and a member of the Center's core group on urban problems.

Morris Janowitz is Professor and Chairman of the Department of Sociology, Director of the Center for Social Organization Studies, and member of the Executive Committee of the Committee for Comparative Study of New Nations, The University of Chicago. He is an authority on civil-military relations, urban problems, intergroup relations, and social change. Mr. Janowitz is the author of, among others, *Competitive Pressures and Democratic Consent* and *Social Change and Prejudice.* He is a Fellow of the Center for Policy Study.

Howard Jenkins, Jr., is a member of the National Labor Relations Board. Formerly Professor of Law at Howard University, he has also served as Special Assistant to the Solicitor, The Department of Labor, and as Assistant Commissioner of the Bureau of Labor-Management Reports.

Frank G. Jennings is Education Consultant of The New World Foundation and Editor-at-Large for *The Saturday Review.* He has taught at The University of Denver, New York University, Yeshiva University, Columbia Teachers College, and Dillard University. Mr. Jennings is a reading specialist and the author of textbooks and numerous articles.

Philip B. Kurland is Professor of Law and a Fellow of the Center for Policy Study, The University of Chicago. He is a specialist on constitutional law and the U.S. Supreme Court. Mr. Kurland is editor of *The Supreme Court Review,* which annually evaluates the Court.

Howard R. Leary, New York City Police Commissioner, served as chief of police in Philadelphia from 1963 until his New York appointment in 1966. His accomplishments in Philadelphia included the appointment of Negroes to high positions within his department and the establishment of a civilian review board, a highly skilled tactical patrol force, and a specially trained civil disobedience squad.

Julian H. Levi is Professor of Urban Studies in the Department of Social Sciences, The University of Chicago, and Executive Director of the South East Chicago Commission. He has been intimately involved in the development and the execution of the Hyde Park–Kenwood urban renewal program. Mr. Levi is author of *Municipal and Institutional Relations Within Boston* and is a Fellow of the Center for Policy Study.

The late *Joseph D. Lohman* was Dean of the School of Criminology, The University of California at Berkeley. He was a former sheriff of Cook County and former Illinois State Treasurer. Dean Lohman was consultant to the Human Resources Research Office, George Washington University, member of the demonstration panel of the President's Committee on Delinquency and Youth Crime, and member of the State of California Advisory Committee on Compensatory Education.

Mayor *Henry W. Maier* of Milwaukee is a member of the Advisory Board of the U.S. Conference of Mayors and of the Executive Committee of the American Municipal Association. He is the author of *Challenge to the Cities*.

Jack Meltzer is Professor and Director of the Center for Urban Studies, The University of Chicago. He is former Director of Planning for The South East Chicago Commission and Michael Reese Hospital. Mr. Meltzer has served as consultant for urban renewal programs throughout the country.

Harold W. Pfautz is Professor in the Department of Sociology and Anthropology, Brown University, and former coordinator of the Tougaloo-Brown Cooperative Program in Mississippi. He is editor of *Charles Booth on the City* and author of articles on social movements and stratification.

Dr. Alvin F. Poussaint is Assistant Professor of Psychiatry at the Tufts University Medical School and former Southern Field Director of the Medical Committee for Human Rights in Jackson, Mississippi. He is the author of articles on minority group psychology.

Walter Pozen, former assistant to the Secretary of the Interior Stewart Udall, is head of the Washington, D.C., office of the law firm Stroock and Stroock and Lavan of New York and Paris. He is co-author of *Strategy for the Sixties* and a member of the Center's core group on urban problems.

Jerome H. Skolnick is Associate Professor of Sociology, The University of Chicago. He is the author of *Justice Without Trial: Law Enforcement in Democratic Society*.

Dr. Jeanne Spurlock was Director of the Child Psychiatric Clinic, Michael Reese Hospital and former Clinical Assistant Professor of Psychiatry at the University of Illinois.

Sol Tax is Professor of Anthropology, The University of Chicago. His major interest is the social anthropology of North and Middle American Indians. Mr. Tax is the author of several books, including *Horizons of Anthropology* and *Evolution After Darwin*. He is a Fellow of the Center for Policy Study.

U.S. Representative *John V. Tunney* of California is a member of the House Committee on Foreign Affairs and on Interior and Insular Affairs. He is a former New York attorney and former member of the faculty of the University of California at Berkeley. He is a member of the Center's core group on urban problems.

Richard C. Wade is Professor in the Department of History and member of the Executive Committee of the Center for Urban Studies, The University of Chicago. He is the author of *Slavery in the Cities* and the forthcoming *Chicago: Growth of a Metropolis.*

FELLOWS OF THE CENTER FOR POLICY STUDY

The following are brief biographies of the Fellows of the Center for Policy Study at The University of Chicago.

Robert McC. Adams

Professor of Anthropology; major scholarly interest is the comparative study of the origin of early civilizations in the Near East and Central America.

George W. Beadle

Director, Institute for Biomedical Research, American Medical Association Educational and Research Fund; President of the University, 1961–68, geneticist; winner of the Nobel Prize (1958) for his work on the chemistry of genes.

Saul Bellow

Professor in the Committee on Social Thought; author of six novels, twice winner of the National Book Award for Fiction (1954, 1964); winner of the International Literary Prize (1965).

Leonard Binder

Professor of Political Science; specialist in the comparative politics of developing nations, in Eastern and Middle Eastern politics and in Islamic culture and political thought.

Walter J. Blum

Professor of Law; specializes in federal taxation, insolvency, and corporate reorganization; co-author of *The Uneasy Case for Progressive Taxation* (1953) and of *Public Law Perspectives on a Private Law Problem: Auto Compensation Plans* (1964).

Jerald C. Brauer

Professor and Dean of the Divinity School; a scholar in the field of church history and Christian thought; author of several books including *Protestantism in America*.

Marshall Cohen

Associate Professor of Philosophy at The Rockefeller University; major scholarly interests are aesthetics, literary criticism, and political and legal philosophy.

Charles U. Daly
University Vice-President for Development and Public Affairs; Director of the Center for Policy Study; former staff assistant to Presidents Johnson and Kennedy; American Political Science Association Congressional Fellow (1959–60).

John Hope Franklin
Professor and Chairman of the Department of History; an authority on the history of the American Negro and on the Civil War and Reconstruction periods; author of a number of books including *From Slavery to Freedom: A History of American Negroes* (1956).

Jacob W. Getzels
Professor of Education and of Psychology; major interests are the social psychology of education and the gifted child; served as consultant to the White House Conference on Education (1965); co-author of *Creativity and Intelligence*.

Julian R. Goldsmith
Professor and Chairman of the Department of Geophysical Sciences, Associate Dean of the Division of the Physical Sciences; member of the Board of the National Science Foundation and of the American Academy of Arts and Sciences.

Chauncy D. Harris
Professor and Chairman of the Department of Geography and Director of the Center for International Studies; major field of interest is economic and urban geography.

Dr. Robert J. Hasterlik
Professor of Medicine; major scholarly field is the study of long-term effects of radium deposits in the human skeleton and means of modifying radium effects; Fellow of the American Association for the Advancement of Science.

Philip M. Hauser
Professor of Sociology; Director of the Population Research Center and the Chicago Community Inventory; formerly Acting Director (1949–50) and Deputy Director (1947–48) of the U.S. Bureau of the Census; authority on population trends.

Ping-ti Ho
James Westfall Thompson Professor of History; major field is the history of modern China; author of four books, including *The Ladder of Success in Imperial China*; co-editor of *China in Crisis*; member of Academia Sinica.

Morris Janowitz
Professor and Chairman of the Department of Sociology and Director of the Center for Social Organization Studies; an authority on civil-military relations, urban problems, intergroup relations, and social change; author of numerous books and publications including *Social Control of Escalated Riots. Competitive Pressures and Democratic Consent, Social Change and Prejdudice,* and *The Community Press in an Urban Setting.*

D. Gale Johnson
Professor of Economics and Dean of the Division of the Social Sciences; major field is agricultural economics, international trade, and Soviet agriculture; has served as consultant to several federal departments and offices.

Philip B. Kurland
Professor of Law; specialist on constitutional law and the U.S. Supreme Court; editor of *The Supreme Court Review*, which annually evaluates the Court; served as law clerk to Justice Felix Frankfurter (1945–46).

Edward H. Levi
President of The University of Chicago; former Provost of the University (1962–68); former Dean of the University's Law School (1950–62); has held several positions with the U.S. government, including Special Assistant to the Attorney General (1940–45); Fellow of the American Bar Foundation and the American Academy of Arts and Sciences.

Julian H. Levi
Professor of Urban Studies; Executive Director of the South East Chicago Commission; has been intimately involved in the development and the execution of the Hyde Park-Kenwood urban renewal program; author of numerous articles on urban planning.

Donald N. Levine
Associate Professor of Sociology and Social Sciences (College); major interests include Ethiopia and sociological theory; author of *Wax and Gold: Tradition and Innovation in Ethiopian Culture.*

Richard C. Lewontin
Professor of Biology and in the Committee on Mathematical Biology; major scholarly interests are population genetics, evolution, and ecology; Associate Dean of the Division of Biological Sciences.

William H. McNeill
Professor of History; author of eight books, including *The Rise of the West* (1963), which won the National Book Award in History; member of the American Academy of Arts and Sciences.

Hans J. Morganthau
Leonard Davis Distinguished Professor in Political Science at City College of New York; author of numerous books including *Politics among Nations* and *Politics in the Twentieth Century.*

William R. Polk
Professor of History and Director of the Center for Middle Eastern Studies; Director of the Adlai Stevenson Institute of International Affairs; former member of the Policy Planning Council of the U.S. Department of State; books include *Backdrop to Tragedy: The Struggle for Palestine* and *The United States and the Arab World.*

Stuart A. Rice
Professor of Chemistry and in the James Franck institute and the Committee on Mathematical Biology; major field of interest is theoretical and experimental chemistry; winner of the American Chemical Society Award in Pure Chemistry and of the Marlow Medal of the Faraday Society of London (1963); member of the Air Force Solid State Physics Panel and of the Office of Aerospace Research Scientific Advisory Group.

Edward A. Shils
Professor of Sociology and in the Committee on Social Thought; Fellow of Kings College, Cambridge University; major scholarly interest is social stratification; editor of *Minerva.*

George P. Shultz
U.S. Secretary of Labor; on academic leave as Professor of Industrial Relations and Dean of the Graduate School of Business; specialist in labor economics, and industrial relations; formerly senior staff economist for the President's Council of Economic Advisers (1955–56).

John A. Simpson
Edward L. Ryerson Distinguished Service Professor of Physics and in the Enrico Fermi Institute; member of the National Academy of Sciences,

discoverer of the third Van Allen radiation belt; member of the committee that planned the International Geophysical Year (1957–58).

George J. Stigler

Charles R. Walgreen Distinguished Service Professor of Economics and in the Graduate School of Business; major interests are industrial organization and the history of economic thought; numerous publications include *Essays in the History of Economics* (1965).

Bernard S. Strauss

Professor of Microbiology; specialist in microbial genetics and mutation; author of *The Outline of Chemical Genetics* (1960) and numerous articles.

Robert E. Streeter

Professor of English and Dean of the Division of the Humanities; specialist in American literature; assisted in reorganizing Korean universities after World War II (1946–47); co-editor of *The Province of Prose* (1956, 1959), a college text.

Sol Tax

Professor of Anthropology; major interest is the social anthropology of North and Middle American Indians; author of several books, including *Horizons of Anthropology* (1963) and *Evolution after Darwin* (1960); editor of *Current Anthropology*.

Tang Tsou

Professor of Political Science; specialist in Sino-American relations; author of *America's Failure in China, 1941–50* (1963), a monograph, *The Embroilment over Quemoy: Mao, Chiang, and Dulles* (1950), and co-editor of *China in Crisis*.

John T. Wilson

Dean of Faculties and Vice-President, The University of Chicago; former Deputy Director of the National Science Foundation; major interests are psychology and human learning.

Albert Wohlstetter

University Professor of Political Science; his research over the past fifteen years has been concerned primarily with methods of deterring nuclear war; an adviser to the Office of the Secretary of Defense and to the U.S. Bureau of the Budget; former Director of Program, National Housing Agency.